Praise for Robert B. Reich and

The Common Good

"Well-argued. . . . A provocative essay."
—*Kirkus Reviews*

"Clear-voiced and accessible."   —*Publishers Weekly*

"Reich is that most exotic of species: an economist who can write."   —*San Francisco Magazine*

"Intriguing. . . . Reich reaches for a vibrant middle, defying easy categorization. You get the sense of original thinking, not rote recital."   —*Barron's*

"Reich has a talent for mastering economic and social complexities and making them easy for the layperson to grasp."   —*The Wall Street Journal*

"[Reich] is calmly articulate, not alarmist; yet a sense of urgency pulses through his unambiguous prose."
—*The Argonaut* (Los Angeles)

Robert B. Reich

The Common Good

Robert B. Reich is Chancellor's Professor of Public Policy at the Goldman School of Public Policy at the University of California, Berkeley. He has served in three national administrations and has written fifteen books, including *The Work of Nations*, *Saving Capitalism*, *Supercapitalism*, and *Locked in the Cabinet*. His articles have appeared in *The New Yorker*, *The Atlantic*, *The New York Times*, *The Washington Post*, and *The Wall Street Journal*. He is cocreator of the award-winning documentary *Inequality for All* and of the Netflix documentary *Saving Capitalism*, and is cofounder of Inequality Media. He lives in Berkeley and blogs at robertreich.org.

Robert B. Reich is available for select speaking engagements. To inquire about a possible appearance, please contact Penguin Random House Speakers Bureau at speakers@penguinrandomhouse.com or visit www.prhspeakers.com.

The
Common Good

The
Common Good

~

Robert B. Reich

VINTAGE BOOKS
A Division of Penguin Random House LLC
New York

The Library of Congress has cataloged the Knopf edition as follows:
Names: Reich, Robert B., author.
Title: The common good / Robert B. Reich.
Description: First edition. New York : Alfred A. Knopf, 2018.
Identifiers: LCCN 2017053384
Subjects: LCSH: Common good. | Citizenship—Moral and
ethical aspects—United States. | Political ethics—United States. |
Economics—Moral and ethical aspects—United States.
Classification: LCC JC330. 15 .R455 2018 | DDC 323.6/50973—dc23
LC record available at https://lccn.loc.gov/2017053384

Vintage Books Trade Paperback ISBN: 978-0-525-43637-9
eBook ISBN: 978-0-525-52050-4

Book design by Maggie Hinders

www.vintagebooks.com

Printed in the United States of America
10   9   8   7   6   5   4   3   2   1

To my dearest Perian

Contents

The
Common Good

Introduction

I WAS AT the impressionable age of fourteen when I heard John F. Kennedy urge us not to ask what America can do for us but what we can do for America. Seven years later I took a job as a summer intern in the Senate office of his brother Robert F. Kennedy. It was not a glamorous job, to say the least. I felt lucky when I was asked to run his signature machine. But I told myself that in a very tiny way I was doing something for the good of the country.

That was a half century ago. I wish I could say America is a better place now than it was then. Surely our lives are more convenient. Fifty years ago there were no cash machines or smartphones, and I wrote my first book on a typewriter. As individuals, we are as kind and generous as ever. We volunteer in our communities, donate, and help one another. We pitch in during natural disasters and emergencies. We come to the aid of individuals in need. We are a more inclusive society, in that African Americans, women, and gays have legal rights they didn't have a half century ago. Yet our civic life—as citizens in our democracy, participants in our economy, managers or employees of companies, and members or leaders of organizations—seems to have sharply deteriorated. What we have lost, I think, is a sense of our connectedness to each other and to our ideals—the America that John F. Kennedy asked that we contribute to.

Starting in the late 1970s, Americans began talking less about the common good and more about self-aggrandizement. The shift is the hallmark of our era: from the "Greatest Generation" to the "Me Generation," from "we're all in it together" to "you're on your own." In 1977, motivational speaker Robert Ringer wrote a book that reached the top of the *New York Times* best-seller list entitled *Looking Out for # 1*. It extolled the virtues of selfishness to a wide and enthusiastic audience. The 1987 film *Wall Street* epitomized the new ethos in the character Gordon Gekko and his signature line, "Greed, for lack of a better word, is good."

The past five decades have also been marked by growing cynicism and distrust toward all of the basic institutions of American society—government, the media, corporations, big banks, police, universities, charities, religious institutions, the professions. There is a wide and pervasive sense that the system as a whole is no longer working as it should. A growing number of Americans feel neglected and powerless. Some are poor, or black or Latino; others are white and have been on a downward economic escalator for years. Many in the middle also feel stressed and voiceless. Whether we call ourselves Democrats or Republicans, liberals or conservatives, we share many of the same anxieties and feel much of the same distrust. We have nonetheless been cleaved into warring ideological tribes, and tribes within those tribes. Some of us have even been seduced by demagogues and conspiracy theorists. We seem to be a long way from when John F. Kennedy asked that Americans contribute to the well-being of all. We no longer even discuss what we owe one another as members of the same society.

As I write this, I am now a septuagenarian and Donald Trump is president. In many ways Trump epitomizes what has gone wrong. But as I hope to make clear, Trump is not the cause. He is a consequence—the logical outcome of what has unfolded over many years. His election was itself propelled by widespread anxieties, and distrust toward our political and economic system. Say what you want about him, Trump has at least brought us back to first principles. Some presidents, like Ronald Reagan, got us talking about the size and role of government. Trump has got us talking about democracy versus tyranny. Some presidents, like Bill Clinton, invited a discussion of how we can make the most of ourselves. Trump, by dint of his pugnacious character and the divisiveness he has fueled, raises the question of what connects us, of what we hold in common.

Hence, this book.

Is there a common good that still binds us together as Americans? That it's even necessary to ask shows how far we've strayed. Today, some think we're connected by the whiteness of our skin, or our adherence to Christianity, or the fact that we were born in the United States. I believe we're bound together by the ideals and principles we share, and the mutual obligations those principles entail.

My hope is that this book provokes a discussion of the good we have had in common, what has happened to it, and what we might do to restore it. Perhaps this book can even provide a means for people with opposing views to debate these questions civilly. My goal is not that we all agree on the common good. It is that we get into the habit and practice of thinking and talking about it, and hearing one another's views about it. This alone would be an advance.

I should clarify from the start what this book is not. It is not about communism or socialism, although in this fractious era I wouldn't be surprised if the word "common" in the title causes some people to assume it is. It is not a book about what progressives or Democrats or Republicans ought to do to win elections, what messages they should convey, or policies they should propose. There is already quite enough advice to go around. And it's not a book about Donald Trump, although he does come up from time to time.

It is a book about what we owe one another as members of the same society—or at least what we did owe one another more than a half century ago when I heard John F. Kennedy's challenge. It is about the good we once had in common—and, if we are to get back to being a far better functioning society, must have again.

PART I

What Is
the Common Good?

CHAPTER 1

Shkreli

BEGIN WITH Martin Shkreli. Pale, thin, and boyish, with dark hair and an impish grin, Shkreli in early life exemplified the rags-to-riches American success story. He was born in Brooklyn, New York, in March 1983, to parents who emigrated from Albania and worked as janitors in New York apartment buildings. Shkreli attended New York's Hunter College High School, a public school for intellectually gifted young people, and in 2004 received a bachelor's degree in business administration from Baruch College. Almost from the start, Shkreli showed a knack for finding unique ways to make lots of money. He started his own hedge fund, betting that the stock prices of certain biotech companies would drop.

But then Shkreli's life story became far less admirable. He used financial chat rooms on the Internet to savage the companies he bet against, causing their prices to drop and his bets to pay off. As one investor recalled, "Shkreli had a really good knowledge of who was faking drug results and who was gaming the system." Another investor remembered he was "willing to take a lot of risk and do things other people won't do." Soon thereafter, Shkreli gained control of a pharmaceutical company called Retrophin, and then, in 2015, he founded and became CEO of another, Turing Pharmaceuticals. Under his direction Turing spent $55 million for the U.S. rights to sell a drug called Daraprim. Developed in 1953, Daraprim is the only approved treatment for toxoplasmosis, a rare parasitic disease that can cause birth defects in unborn babies, and lead to seizures, blindness, and death in cancer patients and people with AIDS. Daraprim is on the World Health Organization's list of Essential Medicines. Months after he bought the rights, Shkreli raised its price by over 5,000 percent, from $13.50 a pill to $750.

Shkreli was roundly criticized for doing this, but he felt justified. "No one wants to say it, no one's proud of it, but this is a capitalist society, a capitalist system and capitalist rules," he explained. "And my investors expect me to maximize profits, not to minimize them or go half or go 70 percent but to go to 100 percent of the profit curve." He claimed he wasn't bothered by the public outcry against him and even wished he had raised the price higher, and said he would buy another drug and raise its price, too. "The attempt to public shame is interesting, because everything we've done is legal. [Standard Oil's John D.] Rockefeller made no attempt to apologize as long as what he was doing was legal." In February 2016, Shkreli was called before a congressional committee to justify his price increase for

Daraprim. He refused to answer any questions, pleading the Fifth Amendment. After the hearing Shkreli tweeted, "Hard to accept that these imbeciles represent the people in our government."

Shkreli was subsequently arrested in connection with an unrelated scheme to defraud his former hedge fund investors by, among other things, sending them fake performance updates after having lost all the fund's money and then hiding the losses by raiding funds from Retrophin, the first company he headed. According to U.S. attorney Robert Capers, Shkreli "essentially ran his companies like a Ponzi scheme," in which he "ensnare[d] investors through a web of lies and deceit." G. Karthik Srinivasan, an assistant U.S. attorney in the Eastern District Court in Brooklyn, said, "Telling lies on top of lies—this is what that man, Martin Shkreli, did for years." In anticipation of his criminal trial, Shkreli boasted to *The New Yorker* magazine, "I think they'll return a not-guilty verdict in two hours. There are going to be jurors who will be fans of mine. I walk down the streets of New York and people shake my hand. They say, 'I want to be just like you.'"

During his trial in the Federal District Court in Brooklyn, Shkreli strolled into a room filled with reporters and made light of a particular witness, for which the trial judge rebuked him. On his Facebook page he mocked the prosecutors, and he told news outlets they were a "junior varsity" team. He retaliated against journalists who criticized him by purchasing Internet domains associated with their names and then mocking them on the sites. "I wouldn't call these people 'journalists,' " he wrote in an email to *Business Insider.* "They are the unwitting recipients of liberalism subsidy from large media and telecom companies," adding that they were "only a few notches above the white supremacists we hear so much about these days." On August 4, 2017, after a five-week trial, Shkreli was convicted on three of eight counts of fraud. Afterward, he called the case "a witch hunt of epic proportions, and maybe they found one or two broomsticks." One of the jurors explained that "Martin Shkreli is his own worst enemy. . . . He could have just said to everyone, 'I lost the money.' But his ego didn't allow him to do that, and that's why he's in the position he is." Initially some of the jurors were concerned about his mental competence, but they concluded that he knew what he was doing.

I chose to begin with Martin Shkreli because his story typifies what has gone wrong. On the basis of the public information we have, what can we reasonably conclude about him? He's obviously smart and driven. It also appears that he'll do whatever it takes to win, regardless of the effects of his behavior on anyone else. He believes that the norms that other people live by don't apply to him. His attitude toward the law is that anything he wants to do is okay unless it is clearly illegal (and even if it's illegal, it's okay if he can get away with it). He shows contempt for anyone who gets in his way—whether judges, prosecutors, or members of Congress. He remains unapologetic for what he has done; presumably he'd do the same in a heartbeat. In all these ways, Martin Shkreli defies what might be called "the common good." But, I ask you, how different is Martin Shkreli from other figures who dominate American life today, even at the highest rungs?

The idea of "the common good" was once widely understood and accepted in America. After all, the U.S. Constitution was designed for "We the people" seeking to "promote the general welfare"—not for "me the selfish jerk seeking as much wealth and power as possible." During the Great Depression of the 1930s and World War II, Americans faced common perils that required us to work together for the common good, and that good was echoed in Franklin D. Roosevelt's "Four Freedoms"—freedom of speech, of worship, from want, and from fear. The common good animated many of us—both white and black Americans—to fight for civil rights and voting rights in the 1960s. It inspired America to create the largest and most comprehensive system of public education the world had ever seen. And it moved many of us to act against the injustice of the Vietnam War, and others of us to serve bravely in that besotted conflict.

Most people are hardwired for some degree of cooperation with and compassion toward others. Human beings would not have survived on earth to this point were we entirely selfish. Some people are downright heroic—consider the first responders to 9/11 and to massive hurricanes; the two bystanders who sought to protect a young Muslim woman from being attacked on a train in Portland, Oregon, in the spring of 2017, and paid with their lives; the thousands of police and firefighters who every day put themselves in harm's way for the good of their communities; the hundreds of thousands of men and women in the armed forces who risk their lives for their country; the whistle-blowers who risk jobs and careers to report misdeeds in business or government; the owners of companies who remain in their communities and keep people employed despite the lure of higher profits elsewhere. You can also see it in everyday altruism among strangers— helping someone lift a stroller up the stairs to a park, calling for medical assistance, aiding a disabled person.

Yet the common good is no longer a fashionable idea. The phrase is rarely uttered today, not even by commencement speakers and politicians. It feels slightly corny and antiquated if not irrelevant. I doubt Martin Shkreli has the slightest idea of what it is. You find growing evidence of a breakdown. You see it in other CEOs who also gouge their customers, loot their corporations, and defraud investors; in athletes involved in doping scandals; in doctors who do unnecessary procedures to collect fatter fees; in lawyers and accountants who look the other way when corporate clients play fast and loose, who even collude with them to skirt the law; in the Wall Street bankers who defrauded their investors and brought the nation to the brink of economic collapse in 2008 before they were bailed out by taxpayers. You find it in police chiefs who look the other way when their officers violate the legal rights of Latinos or African Americans, sometimes injuring or killing them for no reason; in film producers and publicists who choose not to see that a powerful movie mogul they depend on is sexually harassing young women; in politicians who take donations (really, bribes) from wealthy donors and corporations to enact laws their patrons want, or who shutter the government when they don't get the partisan results they seek; and in a president of the United States who lies repeatedly about important issues, refuses to put his financial holdings into a blind trust and then personally profits off his office, and foments racial and ethnic conflict.

The deterioration I'm referring to is sometimes the handiwork of likable men and women who appear to be good-willed and generous but who in reality have no concern for anything beyond their own driving ambition. They, too, will do whatever it takes to win. One day in the spring of 2016, on a corner near my home in Berkeley where I was waiting for the traffic light to change, I began a conversation with a well-dressed man who was also waiting to cross the street. He introduced himself as John Stumpf. His suit and tie seemed so out of place in Berkeley that I asked him what he did for a living. He explained he was CEO of Wells Fargo Bank and was on his way to a meeting. I mentioned that I had been in the Clinton administration and was not a fan of the Wall Street bailout. We decided to continue our conversation and arranged to have a coffee together the following week. I found Stumpf to be charming and self-effacing. He asked me how I thought

Wells Fargo could do a better job letting the public know it wasn't one of those "big bad" Wall Street banks and was making a major effort to be responsible and responsive to its customers and the communities it served. I offered a few ideas, worth no more than the coffee he treated me to. Afterward, I remember thinking how fortunate it was for Wells Fargo to be led by such an admirable person.

A few months later, after news reports of widespread consumer fraud, Wells Fargo admitted to putting millions of its customers' deposits into credit card and bank accounts that the customers had never requested, plunging a number of them into default. As a result of their damaged credit ratings, these customers had to pay an extra $50 million to borrow money. The bank also acknowledged it had charged another half million customers for auto insurance they neither needed nor sought, pushing more than a quarter million of them into delinquency on their car and insurance payments, and leading to nearly 25,000 wrongful vehicle repossessions. The bank had also enrolled thousands of customers in online bill-pay services they never wanted, charging them nearly a million dollars in fees. As if this were not enough, the bank then argued in federal court that its bilked customers had no right to sue the bank as a group, but had to rely on individual arbitration that would likely cost them more in legal fees than any damage reward they might receive.

Before all of this came to light, the bank's top executives—led by Stumpf—ignored the accumulating evidence of fraud. The bank's profits were soaring (it became the fourth most profitable U.S. corporation in 2016). In calls with Wall Street investment analysts, Stumpf repeatedly touted Wells Fargo's ability to sell more and more products to customers. While the frauds were occurring, the value of Stumpf's own stock holdings rose about $200 million. Stumpf was not, it turned out, someone who was concerned about his customers and communities. In many ways, Stumpf was just a more charming version of Martin Shkreli. He was another who had chosen to enrich himself whatever it took, whatever the consequences, the common good be damned.

CHAPTER 2

What Good
Do We Have in Common?

THE COMMON GOOD consists of our shared values about what we owe one another as citizens who are bound together in the same society—the norms we voluntarily abide by, and the ideals we seek to achieve. It is a way of thinking quite opposite to that of Martin Shkreli, John Stumpf, and several other of today's more notorious business and political leaders. A concern for the common good—keeping the common good *in mind*—is a moral attitude. It recognizes that we're all in it together. If there is no common good, there is no society.

Some thinkers and philosophers have attacked the idea of a common good. They argue it's too easily hijacked by dictators and demagogues who want to use it to justify their tyranny and to squelch individual freedom. "The common good is an undefined and undefinable concept," wrote Ayn Rand, a "moral blank check for those who attempt to embody it." When the common good of a society is regarded as something apart from and superior to the individual good of its members, she wrote, "it means that the good of some men takes precedence over the good of others, with those others consigned to the status of sacrificial animals."

Rand was a Russian émigré to the United States whose father's business had been confiscated during the Russian Revolution. Her most influential writing occurred in the 1940s and 1950s, in the shadow of European fascism and Soviet communism. She was best known for two highly popular novels that are still widely read today—*The Fountainhead* (1943) and *Atlas Shrugged* (1957)—and for other writings and interviews in which she expounded her views about what she called the "virtue of selfishness."

Rand saw government actions that require people to give their money and resources to other people under the pretext of a "common good" as steps toward tyranny. She believed that "man exists for his own sake, that the pursuit of his own happiness is his highest moral purpose, that he must not sacrifice himself to others, nor sacrifice others to himself," as she said in a 1964 interview. Medicare, for example, might be desirable for the elderly, she argued, but when others are forced to pay for it they are on ground that could as easily justify "the enslavement, and therefore, the destruction of medical science, the regimentation and disintegration of all medical practice, and the sacrifice of the professional integrity, the freedom, the careers, the ambitions, the achievements, the happiness, the lives of the very men who are to provide that 'desirable' goal—the doctors."

It was far better, in Rand's view, to base society on

autonomous, self-seeking, and self-absorbed individuals. To her, the only community that any of us has in common are family and friends, maintained voluntarily. If we want to be generous, she thought, that's fine, but no one should have the power to coerce us into generosity. And nothing beyond our circle of voluntary associations merits our trust. No institutions or organizations should be able to demand commitments from us. All that can be expected or justified from anyone is selfish behavior, she thought. That behavior is expressed most clearly through the acts of selling what we have to sell and buying what we want to buy in a free market. For her, the common good did not exist.

Rand's philosophy was updated and formalized in 1974 by Harvard philosopher Robert Nozick in his best-selling book *Anarchy, State, and Utopia*. Nozick argued that individual rights are the only justifiable foundation for a society. Instead of a common good, he wrote, "there are only individual people, different individual people, with their own individual lives." For Nozick, it logically followed that "using one of these people for the benefit of others, uses him and benefits the others. Nothing more. . . . Talk of an overall social good covers this up."

When Rand and Nozick propounded these ideas, they seemed quaint if not far-fetched. Anyone who lived through the prior half century had witnessed our interdependence, through depression and war. After the war we had used our seemingly boundless prosperity to finance all sorts of public goods—schools and universities, a national highway system, and health care for the aged and poor (Medicare and Medicaid). We rebuilt war-torn Europe. We sought to guarantee the civil rights and voting rights of African Americans. We opened doors of opportunity to women. Of *course* there was a common good. We were living it.

But then, starting in the late 1970s, Rand's views gained ground. She became the intellectual godmother of modern-day American conservatism, especially its libertarian strand. President Donald Trump once said he identified with Rand's character Howard Roark, in *The Fountainhead,* an architect so upset that a housing project he designed didn't meet specifications he had it dynamited. Others in Trump's circle were influenced by Rand. *Atlas Shrugged* was said to be the favorite book of Rex Tillerson, Trump's secretary of state. Rand also had a major influence on Mike Pompeo, Trump's CIA chief. Trump's first nominee for secretary of labor, Andrew Puzder, said he spent much of his free time reading Rand. The Republican leader of the House of Representatives, Paul Ryan, required his staff to read Rand.

Rand fans are also found at some of the high reaches of American business. Uber's founder and former CEO, Travis Kalanick, has also described himself as a Rand follower. He applied many of her ideas to Uber's code of values. Kalanick even used *The Fountainhead*'s original cover art as his Twitter avatar.

·　　·　　·

I believe Rand, Nozick, and their more modern incarnations are dangerously wrong. Not only does the common good exist, but it is essential for a society to function. Without voluntary adherence to a set of common notions about right and wrong, daily life would be insufferable. We would be living in a jungle where only the strongest, cleverest, and most wary could hope to survive. This would not be a society. It wouldn't even be a civilization, because there would be no civility at its core.

Americans sharply disagree about exactly what we want for America or for the world. But we must agree on basic principles—such as how we deal with our disagreements, the importance of our democratic institutions, our obligations toward the law, and our respect for the truth—if we're to participate in the same society. It's our agreement to these principles that connects us, not agreement about where these principles lead. Edmund Burke, the eighteenth-century British statesman and political thinker who is the philosophical founder of modern conservatism, saw the common good as "the general bank and capital of nations, and of ages." It is the source of civic virtue.

To take the most basic example, we depend on people's widespread and voluntary willingness to abide by laws—not just the literal letter of laws but also the spirit and intent behind them. Consider what would happen if no one voluntarily obeyed the law without first calculating what they could gain by violating it as compared with the odds of the violation being discovered multiplied by the size of the likely penalty. We'd be living in bedlam. If everyone behaved like Martin Shkreli, much of our time and attention would have to be devoted to outwitting or protecting ourselves from others. We would have to assume everyone else was out to exploit us, if they could. Every interaction would need to be carefully hedged. Penalties would need to rise and police enforcement to increase, in order to prevent the Shkrelis among us from calculating they might have more to gain by violating the law and risking the penalty than by abiding it. And because laws can't possibly predict and prevent every potential wrong, they would have to become ever more detailed and exacting in order to prevent the Shkrelis from circumventing them.

Even then we'd be in trouble. We couldn't rely on legislators to block or close loopholes because the Shkrelis would bribe legislators to keep them open, and Shkreli legislators would certainly be open to taking such bribes. Even if we managed to close the loopholes, we couldn't rely on police to enforce the laws because the Shkrelis would bribe the police not to, and Shkreli police would also accept the bribes. Without a shared sense of responsibility to the common good, we would have to assume that everybody—including legislators, judges, regulators, and police—was acting selfishly, making and enforcing laws for their own benefit. I know it's hard to imagine, but even a president of the United States could act like Shkreli.

The followers of Ayn Rand who glorify the "free market" and denigrate "government" are fooling themselves if they think the "free market" gets them off this Shkreli hook. The market is itself a human creation—a set of laws and rules that define what can be owned and traded, and how. Government doesn't "intrude" on the "free market." It *creates* the market. Government officials—legislators, administrators, regulators, judges, and heads of state—must decide on and enforce such laws and rules in order for a market to exist. Without norms for the common good, officials have no way to make these decisions other than their own selfish interests.

Over the years, public officials have decided that you cannot own human beings, nuclear bombs, recipes, or the human genome. You're not permitted to buy sex, babies, or votes. You can't sell dangerous drugs, unsafe foods, or deceptive Ponzi schemes. You mustn't force other people to sell or buy anything from you. By the same token, you have to pay your debts, unless you are allowed to reorganize them under bankruptcy (even then, you're allowed to use bankruptcy only under certain conditions). Other market rules cover everything from what can be copyrighted or patented to whether contracts can require arbitration of disputes, whether specific proposed mergers and acquisitions create too much market power, and whether employment contracts can prevent employees from working for a competitor.

Hopefully, government officials base these sorts of decisions on their notions about the common good. But if Shkrelis were making and enforcing such rules, they'd be based on whatever it took for these Shkreli officials to gain personal wealth and power. The "free market" would be a sham, and most people would lose out in it. (As we will see in the pages to come, something close to this has in fact occurred.)

Truth itself is a common good. Through history, one of the first things tyrants have done is attack independent truth-tellers—philosophers (Plato), scientists (Galileo), and the free and independent press—thereby confusing the public and substituting their own "facts." Without a shared truth, democratic deliberation is hobbled. "Alternative facts" are an open invitation to what George Orwell described as "doublethink," in which the public is so confused it cannot recall the past, assess the present, or contemplate the future. As poet and philosopher Václav Havel put it, "If the main pillar of the system is living a lie, then it is not surprising that the fundamental threat to it is living in truth."

Yet in a world populated by people like Martin Shkreli, we could not trust anyone to be truthful if they could do better for themselves by lying. We couldn't count on any claim by sellers of any product or service. Internet-based "reputational ratings" would be of little value because Shkreli raters would be easily bribed. Transparency would be impossible because Shkrelis would hide the truth and mess with all indicators of it. Journalists would shade their reports for their own selfish advantage, taking bribes from advertisers or currying favor with politicians. Teachers would offer lessons to satisfy wealthy or powerful patrons. Historians would alter history if by doing so they gained wealth or power. Scientists would doctor evidence for similar selfish motives. The truth would degenerate into a cacophony of competing factual claims.

We couldn't trust doctors or pharmacists to give us the right medications. We couldn't trust bankers and accountants not to fleece us, restaurants not to poison us, lawyers not to hoodwink us. All ratings would be gamed. Professional ethics would be meaningless. If we couldn't believe anything we heard, we would find ourselves in a permanent state of bewilderment. As Augustine said, "Nothing at all of human society remains safe, if we shall determine to believe nothing, which we cannot grasp by full apprehension."

The common good is especially imperiled when a president of the United States alleges that millions of unauthorized immigrants voted illegally, when there's no evidence they did; that the news media cover up terrorism by Islamic extremists, when nothing suggests they do; that his predecessor in office illegally wiretapped him, when no facts back up such a claim; and that his journalistic critics peddle "fake news," without evidence of such duplicity. Such baseless claims mislead and confuse the public. They erode trust. They fuel conspiracy theories. They can lead to a vicious cycle in which opportunists use the prevailing distrust to propagate more lies, for their own purposes. Alex Jones, best known for suggesting 9/11 was an inside job and the Sandy Hook Elementary School shooting was "completely fake," has said, "The public doesn't have any trust in the system. They believe the social contract is broken"—which is exactly what has enabled people like Jones to gain influence.

·   ·   ·

Most basically, the common good depends on people trusting that most others in society will also adhere to the common good, rather than lie or otherwise take advantage of them. In this way, civic trust is self-enforcing and self-perpetuating. As James Madison put it when advocating the Bill of Rights, the mere knowledge of its existence would "extinguish from the bosom of every member of the community any apprehensions, that there are those among his countrymen who wish to deprive them of the liberty for which they valiantly fought and honorably bled."

History has shown that the more commitment to the common good there is within a society, the more willing are its inhabitants to accept disruptions that inevitably accompany new ideas, technologies, opportunities, trade, and immigration. That's because these inhabitants are more likely to trust that the disruptions won't unfairly burden them, and that they stand to gain more than lose by them. This sort of virtuous circle is more likely in societies that promote political equality and equal opportunity, because people who have an equal voice in setting the rules and an equal chance to get ahead naturally feel more assured that their concerns will be addressed and that changes can work to their advantage.

But when that trust is undermined or was never there to begin with, disruptive change can generate widespread anger and fear, and even political upheaval. Under these circumstances, virtuous circles can reverse themselves and become vicious cycles. If those who feel left behind view the system as rigged against them, they can push open societies into becoming closed and autocratic. Where a sense of common good is lacking, demagogues can use the anger and fear accompanying disruptive change to turn people against one another rather than address the traumas that made them angry in the first place. Societies experiencing economic stresses and widening inequalities are particularly vulnerable to tyrants intent on undermining democratic institutions by lying repeatedly, accusing critics of conspiring against "the people," fueling racial and ethnic divisions, and inciting rabid nationalism.

Polls tell us that a majority of today's Americans worry that the nation is losing its national identity. The core of that identity has never been "we're better than anyone else" nationalism. Nor has it been the whiteness of our skin or the uniformity of our ethnicity. Our core identity—the most precious legacy we have been given by the generations who came before us—is the ideals we share, the good we hold in common. If we are losing our national identity, it is not because we are becoming browner or speak in more languages than we once did. It is because we are losing our sense of the common good.

"We're better than anyone else" nationalism, tinged with racism, typically emerges in countries where demagogues build their base of power by fueling fears of others outside the nation's borders. The assertion made in 2017 by Marine Le Pen, leader of France's National Front, that the major political contest in today's world is between global-ism and patriotism, was nothing but fear-based nativism. So was Donald Trump's "America First" rallying cry in the 2016 presidential election, which echoed earlier nativist calls in America (in the 1850s, 1890s, and 1920s) for the nation to shut itself off from the rest of the world. In contrast to John F. Kennedy's call to put selfishness aside and invest more of ourselves in the common good, Trump called on Americans to prevent the rest of the world from encroaching on us. "We will ... not allow other countries to take advantage of us like they've been doing to a level that's hard to believe," he said in his surly inauguration speech. "Nobody—nobody—can beat us. Nobody. We are Americans, and the future belongs to us." Early in his administration, Trump's foreign policy team flatly rejected the idea that the world is a "global community," in favor of the zero-sum fallacy that the world is "an arena where nations, nongovernmental actors, and businesses engage and compete for advantage."

But we are not in a zero-sum game with the rest of the world. Our common good is inextricably bound up in the good of the rest of the planet. America understood this explicitly in the decades after World War II when we helped rebuild war-torn Europe and Japan. To be sure, at least since the end of World War II, America has sought to be the world's leading superpower. But not until Trump has an administration viewed other nations' gains as our losses, and vice versa. The common good has nothing whatever to do with the United States being "the best." It's not about securing borders, erecting walls, and keeping others out. It is not xenophobic. It doesn't focus on exclusion at all. To the contrary, the common good is about *inclusion*—joining together to achieve common goals.

In fact, it is by coming together for the common good that we gain compassion for others beyond a nation's borders. As Edmund Burke put it, "To be attached to the subdivision, to love the little platoon we belong to in society, is the first principle (the germ as it were) of public affections. It is the first link in the series by which we proceed toward a love to our country and to mankind." Burke, long a hero to American conservatives, was no nationalist. He devoted most of his career to defending oppressed groups around the world, such as American colonists who were being exploited by his own British compatriots; Irish Catholics, who were being discriminated against; and the masses of India. In so doing, Burke did not base his arguments on universal principles of human rights. He based them on moral precepts underlying Britain's own laws and unwritten constitution.

"We're better than anyone else" nationalists typically don't know or care about the rest of the world. As George Orwell dryly observed, a nationalist, "although endlessly brooding on power, victory, defeat, revenge, is typically uninterested in what happens in the real world." True patriots, by contrast, are deeply curious about, and open to, the rest of humanity. Their sense of the common good doesn't end at the nation's borders. Daniel Fried, who joined the U.S. Foreign Service in 1977 and served America with distinction for forty years, said on his retirement in

February 2017, "We are not in an ethno-state, with identity rooted in shared blood. The option of a White Man's Republic ended at Appomattox. . . . We have, imperfectly, and despite detours and retreats along the way, sought to realize a better world for ourselves and for others, for we understood that our prosperity and our values at home depend on that prosperity and those values being secure as far as possible in a sometimes dark world."

America's original sin was not the exclusion of people born outside the nation's borders from citizenship. It was the exclusion of many people who had lived here even before the start of the Republic—in particular, Native Americans and African Americans. For most of its existence, America found it relatively easy to assimilate foreigners, although there were periods of sharp and even violent tension. By the 1840s, every major seaport teemed with inhabitants from around the globe—"Feegeeans, Tongatobooarrs, Erromanggoans, Pannangians, and Brighggians," and other "wild specimens of the whaling-craft," as Herman Melville described the streets of New Bedford, Massachusetts, in *Moby-Dick*. Until the early 1920s, almost anyone could come to America and become a citizen. Yet from its inception, America refused to include Native Americans and African Americans as equal citizens. In *Dred Scott v. Sandford* (1857), a majority of the Supreme Court shamefully held that African Americans could not become the fellow citizens of white Americans because they were "beings of an inferior order, and altogether unfit to associate with the white race."

Dred Scott was overruled, but the fight for equal justice

in America—for a more inclusive "We the people"—has continued. That fight, too, is part of the common good. The poems of Walt Whitman and Langston Hughes, and the songs of Woody Guthrie, express loving devotion to America—while turning that love into a demand for justice. "This land is your land, this land is my land" sang Guthrie. "Let America be America again," pleaded Hughes: "The land that never has been yet— / And yet must be—the land where every man is free. / The land that's mine— the poor man's, Indian's, Negro's, ME—."

Patriotism based on the common good does not pander to divisiveness. True patriots don't fuel racist or religious or ethnic divisions. They aren't homophobic or sexist or racist. To the contrary, true patriots confirm the good that we have in common. They seek to strengthen and celebrate the "We" in "We the people."

A love of country based on the common good entails obligations to other people, not to national symbols. Instead of demanding displays of respect for the flag and the anthem, it requires that all of us take on a fair share of the burdens of keeping the nation going—that we pay taxes in full rather than seek tax loopholes or squirrel away money abroad, that we volunteer time and energy to improving the community and country, serve on school boards and city councils, refrain from political contributions that corrupt our politics, and blow the whistle on abuses of power even at the risk of losing our jobs. It has sometimes required the supreme sacrifice. We are the descendants of Nathan Hale, soldier and spy for the Continental Army during the Revolutionary War, who famously declared just before being executed by the British in 1776 that his only regret was having "but one life to lose for my country." Franklin D. Roosevelt, in the midst of the Great Depression of the 1930s, called upon America's wellspring of generosity and sacrifice for the good of all. "If I read the temper of our people correctly," he said,

> we now realize as we have never realized before our interdependence on each other; that we cannot merely take but we must give as well; that if we are to go forward, we must move as a trained and loyal army willing to sacrifice for the good of a common discipline, because without such discipline no progress is made, no leadership becomes effective. We are, I know, ready and willing to submit our lives and property to such discipline, because it makes possible a leadership which aims at a larger good.

This sense of a common good also embraces public education—but not as a personal investment in getting a good job after one's education is complete. Education is a public good that builds the capacity of a nation to wisely govern itself, and promotes equal opportunity. Democracy depends on citizens who are able to recognize the truth, analyze and weigh alternatives, and civilly debate their future, just as it depends on citizens who have an equal voice and equal stake in it. Without an educated populace, a common good cannot even be discerned. This is fundamental. When education is viewed as a private investment yielding private returns, there is no reason why anyone other than the "investor" should pay for it. But when understood as a public good underlying our democracy, all of us have a responsibility to ensure that it is of high quality, and available to all.

Our central obligation as citizens is to preserve, fortify, and protect our democratic form of government—not inundate it with big money and buy off politicians. We must defend the right to vote and ensure that *more* citizens are heard, not fewer. We can't hate our government, for it is the means by which we can come together to help solve our common problems. We may not like everything the government does, and we justifiably worry when special interests gain too much power over it, but our obligation is to work to improve government, not undermine it.

Although Americans have strong disagreements about the size and scope of government, most of us still believe in our *system* of government. We're often angry and disappointed at how far it falls short of our ideals, and we can be incensed when the system appears to be rigged against us, but most of us agree with its ideals, and we're angry at the riggers—not at the system. As citizens, we are committed to the Constitution and the rule of law, to democracy based on the consent of the governed. We're committed to the Bill of Rights; to an independent judiciary; separation of powers between the executive, the legislature, and the courts; and in checks and balances among those three branches. We believe in federalism, giving states and localities significant responsibilities. We believe in freedom of speech. We are committed to a free and independent press. Importantly, most of us believe in political equality. We believe that citizens should have an equal right to vote, and that no one's vote should count more than anyone else's. We believe in equality before the law, and that no one should be above the law. We don't want government to discriminate against racial or ethnic minorities.

The genius of a system based on political equality is that it doesn't require us to agree on every issue, but only agree to be bound by decisions that emerge from the system. Some of us may want to prohibit abortions because we believe life begins at conception; others of us believe women should have the right to determine what happens to their bodies. Some of us want stricter environmental protections; others, more lenient. We are free to take any particular position on these and any other issues. But as political equals, we are bound to accept the outcomes even if we dislike them. This requires enough social trust for us to regard the views and interests of those with whom we disagree as equally worthy of consideration to our own. As philosopher John Rawls has written, "Questions of justice and fairness arise when free persons, who have no authority over one another, are participating in their common institutions and among themselves settling or acknowledging the rules which define them and which determine the resulting shares in their benefits and burdens."

· · ·

Ayn Rand had it completely wrong. Moral choices logically involve duties to others, not just calculations about what's best for ourselves. When members of a society ask, "What is the right or decent thing to do?," they necessarily draw upon understandings of these mutual obligations. While our contemporary culture of self-promotion, iPhones, selfies, and personal branding churns out a fair number of narcissists, it is our loyalties and attachments that define who we are.

CHAPTER 3

The Origins of the Common Good

IT IS IMPORTANT not to romanticize the past. As I've noted, at America's founding the common good did not include African Americans or Native Americans. Women and the nonpropertied poor could not vote. The founding fathers nonetheless embraced a set of principles that would eventually lead to a far more inclusive society. They understood that the best way to preserve freedom was through people fiercely committed to it. When they spoke of "virtue," it was not as we understand the term, involving personal kindness and generosity. For them, virtue meant a concern for the common good. Without a virtuous citizenry, they feared the young republic would succumb to authoritarian rule.

They didn't try to create the most efficient system of governance, or one that would generate the most wealth. They wanted a system that would produce the most virtuous people. "Is there no virtue among us?" asked James Madison, rhetorically. "If there be not, no form of government can render us secure. To suppose that any form of government will secure liberty or happiness without any virtue in the people is a chimerical idea." In *Federalist No. 71*, Madison wrote that "it is a just observation that the people commonly INTEND the PUBLIC GOOD" (emphasis in the original), and in *Federalist No. 45* he claimed that "the public good, the real welfare of the great body of the people, is the supreme object to be pursued; and that no form of government whatever has any other value than as it may be fitted for the attainment of this object."

Both Madison and Thomas Jefferson were influenced by the eighteenth-century French Enlightenment philosopher Montesquieu, who defined a "republic" as a self-regulating political society whose mainspring was civic virtue. Edmund Burke likewise noted the connection between a virtuous citizenry and the prevention of tyranny. In his "Thoughts on the Cause of the Present Discontents" (1770), Burke warned that "when bad men combine, the good must associate; else they will fall one by one, an unpitied sacrifice in a contemptible struggle." Almost two centuries later, Martin Luther King, Jr., applied the same logic to the struggle for civil rights in America. "The ultimate tragedy is not the oppression and cruelty by the bad people but the silence over that by the good people."

When Frenchman Alexis de Tocqueville visited the United States in the 1830s, he attributed the strength of America's young democracy to the "habits of the heart," as he called them—the "sum of moral and intellectual dispositions" that emerged from Americans' experience in self-government. It was through governing themselves that Americans learned to put public responsibility over selfish interest. "Citizens who are bound to take part in public affairs must turn from their private interests and occasionally take a look at something other than themselves," Tocqueville wrote. The New Englander, for example, "invests his ambition and his future" in his town, and "accumulates clear, practical ideas about the nature of his duties and the extent of his rights."

The public-spiritedness of New Englanders was replicated across America in barn-raisings and quilting bees. It can still be observed in neighbors who volunteer as firefighters or help one another during natural disasters, whose generosity erects the local hospital and propels high school achievers to college, and who send their young men and women off to fight wars for the good of all. It is found in America's tradition of civic improvement, philanthropy, and local boosterism. Popular culture once echoed these sentiments without sounding corny or inauthentic. They could be found in Robert Sherwood's plays, the novels of John Steinbeck and William Saroyan, Aaron Copland's music, and Frank Capra's films. The last scene in *It's a Wonderful Life* conveys the lesson: George Bailey, played by Jimmy Stewart, learns that he can count on his neighbors, just as they had always counted on him. They are bound together in the common good.

The good that emerged from self-government was not mainly about generosity toward those in need. It was about giving others an equal chance to succeed. In 1892, social reformer Jane Addams explained that Hull House, her settlement house in a poor precinct of Chicago, was not a charity. Hull House's purpose—and, for Addams, a central obligation of American citizenship—was to help America's less fortunate make the most of themselves. "To call this effort philanthropy is to use the word unfairly and to underestimate the duties of good citizenship," she said. Giving others an equal opportunity was an essential aspect of the common good. Martin Luther King, Jr., enunciated the same ideal when he spoke on the National Mall in 1963 about a vision of equal rights "deeply rooted in the American Dream."

Some of our ideas about what we owe each other are also rooted in the Old and New Testaments of the Bible. In the earliest days of Christianity, a church father named John Chrysostom (c. 347–407) wrote: "This is the rule of most perfect Christianity, its most exact definition, its highest point, namely, the seeking of the common good . . . for nothing can so make a person an imitator of Christ as caring for his neighbors." America began as a nation of religious communities whose members pledged to piety and charity and to the good of each other. The highest goal of the Puritans who landed in New England was to create communities fostering ethical and spiritual values. John Winthrop, elected the first governor of the Massachusetts Bay Colony even before the Puritans left England, delivered on board their ship in Salem Harbor, just before they landed in 1630, a sermon that described the effort on which they were embarking in terms of Matthew's version of the Sermon on the Mount. "We must delight in each other, make others' conditions our own, rejoice together, mourn together, labor and suffer together, always having before our eyes... our community as members of the same body." Winthrop saw freedom not as a license to satisfy selfish wants but to do that "which is good, just and honest."

Other ideas about what we owe one another originated in legal compacts dating back to the Babylonian Code of Hammurabi from Mesopotamia, around 1750 BC, and to Roman law and the principles of *civis romanus sum* ("I am a Roman citizen"). Although many inhabitants of these ancient societies were serfs or slaves without rights of citizenship, those who gained citizenship pledged to treat other citizens as equals under the law. In the eleventh and twelfth centuries, various European cities came into existence through similar acts of oath-taking and contract-making. The Flemish charter of Aire promised that each would "help the other like a brother." As the perimeters of citizenship expanded—from the Magna Carta (1215), to the British Bill of Rights (1689), to the U.S. Constitution (1787)—so did these ideas about equal political rights and mutual obligation. None of these expansions came easily; many necessitated harsh struggle and at times troubling compromise. Women did not get the right to vote in the

United States until 1920. Despite the Civil Rights Act of 1965, many blacks today are still effectively denied the equal rights of citizenship and equal opportunity. Same-sex couples eventually gained equal marriage rights in 2015. America continues to engage in a fierce debate over which immigrants to our shores should be granted citizenship, and how noncitizens should be treated.

Our compact is not just with those who are alive today. It's also with those who have come before us and those yet to be born. To the founding fathers, the Constitution and our system of government established a moral bond connecting generations. "There seems . . . to be some foundation in the nature of things, in the relation which one generation bears to another, for the *descent* of obligations from one to another," wrote James Madison. "Equity may require it. Mutual good may be promoted by it. And all that seems indispensable in stating the account between the dead and the living is to see that the debts against the latter do not exceed the advances made by the former." The young Abraham Lincoln understood this moral bond explicitly: "We find ourselves under the government of a system of political institutions, conducting more essentially to the ends of civil and religious liberty, than any of which the history of former times tell us," he said in his first important public speech, in 1838. "We, when mounting the stage of existence, found ourselves the legal inheritors of these fundamental blessings. We toiled not in the acquirement or establishment of them—they are a legacy bequeathed to us, by a once hardy, brave, and patriotic, but now lamented and departed race of ancestors." Twenty-three years later, in his first inaugural address, Lincoln referred to it as America's "mystic chords of memory," a covenant linking past and future.

It was that covenant—not any particular race, religion, or ethnicity—that gave America its ideals and identity. "The American trick," political philosopher Benjamin Barber has noted, "was to use the fierce attachments of patriotic sentiment to bond a people to high ideals." The "tribal" sources from which we derive our sense of national identity, Barber argues, are the documents and statements that enunciate those ideals—the Declaration of Independence, the Constitution and the Bill of Rights, the inaugural addresses of some of our presidents, Lincoln's Gettysburg Address, and Martin Luther King, Jr.'s, "free at last" sermon at the 1963 March on Washington. These documents and statements themselves don't bind us; it's the sentiments behind them that do. They connect us with the ideals and responsibilities espoused by previous generations. They remind us to leave them to future generations.

These generational attachments form the tacit subtext of our daily conversations about American life, permeating *both* American conservatism and American liberalism, and the essential point is that they are fundamentally noble, essentially life-affirming sentiments. Much is made of the American political distinctiveness of a Constitution inspired by theory rather than by tradition. But there is a subtler yet equally profound *cultural* distinctiveness as well, a national sense of identity rooted in a history of self-told mythology. Political scientist Carl Friedrich captured the distinction in 1935: "To be an American is an ideal, while to be a Frenchman is a fact." That idealism led Lincoln to proclaim that America might yet be the "last best hope" for humankind. It prompted Emma Lazarus, some two decades later, to welcome to America the world's "tired, your poor / Your huddled masses yearning to breathe free." It inspired Scottish immigrant Frances Wright—feminist, abolitionist, and advocate of free public education—to write, "What is it to be an American? Is it to have drawn the first breath in Maine, in Pennsylvania, in Florida, or in Missouri? Pshaw! Hence with such paltry, pettifogging calculations of nativities! They are Americans who have complied with the constitutional regulations of the United States . . . wed the principles of America's declaration to their hearts and render the duties of American citizens practically to their lives." And it allowed Supreme Court justice Hugo Black to sum up America's sense of the common good as a "constitutional faith."

To summarize, the good we have had in common has been a commitment to respecting the rule of law, including its intent and spirit; to protecting our democratic institutions; to discovering and spreading the truth; to being open to change and tolerant of our differences; to ensuring equal political rights and equal opportunity; to participating in our civic life together, and sacrificing for that life together. Note that these are not the constitutional rights and freedoms we possess as citizens. They are the essential elements of what we owe one another as Americans. We passionately disagree about all manner of things. But we must share these commitments to each other because they are—or have been—what makes us a *people*. Although we have often fallen short of achieving them, they are ideals that we have strived to realize. They have informed our judgments about right and wrong, decisions we make that could affect others, and our understanding of our obligations as citizens. They have bound us together. They are large and noble obligations.

The central moral question of our age is whether we are still committed to them.

PART II

What Happened
to the Common Good?

CHAPTER 4

Exploitation

LET ME PUT IT THIS WAY: The common good is a pool of trust built up over generations, a trust that most other people share the same basic ideals I've just discussed. This pool of trust has great value. It makes everyone's lives simpler and more secure. But precisely because it has so much value and is maintained voluntarily, it has been possible for some individuals to exploit it for their own selfish gain.

In any social system it's possible to extract benefits by being among the first to break widely accepted unwritten rules. Think about a small town where people don't lock their doors or windows because of the unwritten rule that no one steals. Under these circumstances, the first thief to commit robberies operates at a huge advantage. He can effortlessly get into anyone's house. That first-mover advantage disappears as soon as people catch on and start locking their doors and windows.

Modern societies are filled with tacit rules that can be exploited by people who view them as opportunities for selfish gain rather than as social constraints. "I never thought anyone could do that" is the typical response of everyone else—to whom it literally never occurred that someone would take advantage of the unwritten rule. But after the exploitation occurs, the rule inevitably changes to the equivalent of "people do steal, so lock your doors and windows." Thereafter everyone else has to take steps—often inconvenient, time-consuming, or costly in other ways—to prevent the exploitation from recurring.

Sometimes laws have to become far more detailed and complex. The first high-priced tax attorney to discover an ambiguous provision in the tax code that allows his wealthy client to save a bundle has a first-mover advantage, until the code is amended with a more detailed provision blocking the maneuver. But as a result, everyone thereafter has to grapple with a tax code that's a bit more complicated. Multiply this by every high-priced tax attorney looking for ambiguous provisions and you discover why the tax code has become as complicated as it is.

Trust can disappear altogether. If honest used car dealers can't differentiate themselves from dishonest ones, they may figure there's no point in making sure their cars are reliable. Eventually, no one trusts used car dealers. If a few members of Congress retire to become well-paid lobbyists for industries they once oversaw, other members of Congress will have fewer qualms about doing the same. Eventually, so many turn to lobbying that the public stops trusting members of Congress to act in the common good when they're in office.

If exploitation isn't contained, competitive forces can erode standards. After one pharmaceutical company jacks up the price of a life-saving drug, CEOs of competing companies with life-saving drugs will be pressured by their investors to do the same. If one corporation awards its CEO an unprecedented large pay package, other companies will be under pressure to match it. Political standards can similarly erode. If a candidate is elected because she broke the unwritten rule not to flood the Internet with fake information about her opponent, future candidates will feel less hesitant to flood the Internet with fake information. If a presidential candidate refuses to release his tax returns and suffers no consequence, future candidates will feel less obliged to release theirs. Once norms are broken without consequence, further breakage ensues.

If there are no consequences, norm-breakers can reap enormous gains while the costs of the norm-breaking are shifted to everyone else—locks that have to be purchased; laws that have to become more detailed; monitors, accountants, and security personnel who must be hired; added red tape that hobbles all transactions; and the enmity and distrust that can begin to envelop an entire economic and political system.

Several years ago political scientist James Q. Wilson noted that a broken window in a poor community, left unattended, signals that no one cares if windows are broken there. Because nobody is concerned enough to enforce the norm against breaking windows, the broken window becomes a kind of invitation to throw more stones and break more windows. As more windows shatter, other aspects of community life also start unraveling. The unspoken norm becomes: Do whatever you want here because everyone else is doing it.

The "broken window" theory has led to such picayune and arbitrary law enforcement that it has failed many poor communities. Meanwhile, law enforcers have often disregarded the largest windows in our society that have been shattered by the most prominent stone throwers. As I shall show, around five decades ago a few people with wealth and power began exploiting social trust in order to gain even more wealth and power. Then, seeing how easily it was done and how richly they were rewarded, others followed. The exploiters said, in effect: "I'm going to amass as much wealth and power as I can, whatever it takes. Being decent and responsible is for losers." As America produced a wave of Martin Shkrelis, the unwritten rules that once defined and enforced the common good began to erode.

Here's a rough timeline of the breakdown since the mid-1960s.*

1964 *Gulf of Tonkin.* Lyndon Johnson justifies a
        sharp escalation of the Vietnam War by falsely

---

* With thanks to Hugh Heclo, who includes some of these scandals in *On Thinking Institutionally.*

claiming that North Vietnam launched an "unprovoked attack" against a U.S. destroyer on "routine patrol" in the Gulf of Tonkin, followed by a "deliberate attack" on a pair of U.S. ships.

1971 *The Pentagon Papers.* A leaked Defense Department report shows that while the Johnson administration promised not to expand the Vietnam War, it secretly did so.

1971 *Lewis Powell memo.* The future Supreme Court justice summons business leaders to use their economic muscle aggressively to gain political influence.

1972–74 *Watergate.* The headquarters of the Democratic National Committee at the Watergate complex in Washington, D.C., is broken into by a covert operation set up by Richard Nixon's White House, followed by cover-ups by Nixon and his top assistants. Nixon also maintains an "enemies" list and uses the FBI to harass those on the list.

1980 *The Abscam scandal.* After an FBI sting operation, seven members of Congress are convicted of accepting bribes in return for various political favors.

1985 *Carl Icahn makes a hostile takeover of TWA.* The raider then sells TWA's assets to repay the debt he used to purchase the company.

1986–95 *The Savings and Loan scandals.* More than 1,000 out of 3,234 savings and loan banks fail, at a total cost to taxpayers of $132.1 billion. Several politicians are implicated for taking bribes.

1986–87 *The Iran-contra scandal.* President Ronald Reagan's national security team conspires to sell American weapons to the Iranian Revolutionary Guard and, after marking up the price fivefold, skims the proceeds of those sales and gives them to the anticommunist contra rebels in Nicaragua. This is a direct violation of federal law cutting off aid to the rebels. Reagan initially denies it occurred. Several years later, President George H. W. Bush pardons the major Iran-contra perpetrators before their criminal trials are scheduled to start.

1987 *Robert Bork's rejection.* After a vicious confirmation battle over Republican Bork's nomination to the Supreme Court, he is defeated by virulent partisan opposition.

1990 *Michael Milken conviction.* The corporate raider, who headed the junk bond division of the Wall Street investment firm Drexel Burnham Lambert, is convicted following a guilty plea on felony charges for violating U.S. securities laws.

1991 *Keating Five scandal.* Five senators are found to have obstructed an investigation of the savings and loan industry after they received political contributions from these businesses. (In 1989, Democratic House majority whip Tony Coelho resigned from Congress after revelations of

unethical conduct involving the savings and
loan industry and junk bonds.)

1992 *House banking scandal.* House members are
found to have benefited from special banking
privileges. Four former congressmen are
convicted of criminal wrongdoing.

1993–98 *Whitewater scandal.* Charges of illegal
activities involving land deals financed by the
Clintons during the 1980s lead to convictions
of several Clinton friends, business associates, a
municipal judge, and the governor of Arkansas.

1995 *Dan Rostenkowski scandal.* House Ways and
Means Committee chairman Rostenkowski is
convicted of embezzlement.

1995 *United Way scandal.* The charity's longtime
national CEO, William Aramony, and two other
top officials are convicted of stealing from it
to support lavish lifestyles. Several other local
United Way CEOs are subsequently convicted
of stealing from the charity.

1995 *Government shutdown.* A breakdown in
negotiations between President Bill Clinton and
House Speaker Newt Gingrich over the federal
budget causes the first-ever shutdown of the
entire federal government.

1997–98 *Newt Gingrich reprimand.* The House
reprimands and fines House Speaker Gingrich
for improper financial deals. He subsequently
resigns.

1998 *The Rampart scandal.* Widespread corruption in the Los Angeles Police Department's antigang unit implicates more than seventy police officers for unprovoked beatings, planting false evidence, unprovoked shootings, stealing and dealing narcotics, bank robbery, perjury, and covering up evidence of these activities.

1998–99 *Clinton impeachment.* Bill Clinton is impeached for perjury and obstruction of justice for falsely testifying that he did not have sexual relations with a White House intern. Clinton is then acquitted in the Senate trial.

1999 *Financial derivatives.* The Clinton administration is asked by the chairman of the Commodity Futures Trading Commission to regulate financial "derivatives." Pressured by Wall Street, the administration refuses.

1999 *Repeal of the Glass-Steagall Act.* Clinton joins with congressional Republicans in repealing the act, which since the 1930s had separated commercial banking from investment banking.

2000–2007 *Wall Street gambles.* Taking advantage of deregulation, major Wall Street banks underwrite risky mortgages, mix them in with safe securities, and resell the packages to unsuspecting investors. Major credit-rating agencies, eager to maintain their relationships with the banks, give the packages AAA ratings.

2001 *The war against terrorism.* Five days after the

September 11 attacks, Vice President Dick
Cheney warns that the White House will need
to go over to "the dark side" to fight al Qaeda.
Among the dark places the White House goes
are a top secret program code-named Stellar
Wind, under which the National Security
Agency eavesdrops freely in the United States
without search warrants, and the use of torture
on suspects, in violation of the Geneva Accords.

2001 *Red Cross scandal.* In the wake of the attacks,
the Red Cross raises more than a half billion
dollars, promising all donations will go to
victims and their families. A congressional
investigation reveals that roughly half of the
donations are reallocated to other operations
of the Red Cross. Red Cross's head, Bernadine
Healy, resigns.

2001–2002 *Corporate looting and inside-information
scandals.* Several major companies including
Adelphia, Tyco, WorldCom, and Enron fake
profits and hide debt off the books. Former
Enron CEO Jeffrey Skilling is sentenced to
prison. Businesswoman and TV personality
Martha Stewart serves a brief prison sentence
for insider trading.

2002 *Arthur Andersen scandal.* The accounting
firm is convicted of obstruction of justice for
shredding Enron-related documents. The firm
subsequently folds.

2002 *Auction house price-fixing scandal.* Sotheby's and Christie's auction houses, controlling 90 percent of the high-end auction market, are found to have engaged in a price-fixing conspiracy. Sotheby's chairman, billionaire Alfred Taubman, is fined and jailed.

2003 *Dot-com bubble scandals.* After the "dot-com bubble" bursts, the SEC finds that every major U.S. investment bank assisted in efforts to defraud investors, such as urging them to buy shares in dot-com companies that the banks' own analysts were privately describing as junk. All leading public accounting firms admit negligence in executing their duties, and pay fines.

2003 *Weapons of mass destruction.* The George W. Bush administration claims that Saddam Hussein's regime has weapons of mass destruction, as the reason for invading Iraq. No such weapons are ever found.

2005 *Jack Abramoff scandal.* Political lobbyists Abramoff and Michael Scanlon overbill Native American tribes seeking to develop casino gambling on their reservations, and give gifts and campaign donations to members of Congress in return for votes. Representative Bob Ney and two aides to Tom DeLay are directly implicated.

2007 *Goldman Sachs conflict of interest.* While

promoting risky mortgage-related securities
to its clients, Goldman Sachs places large bets
against those same securities.

2008 *Bear Stearns goes belly-up.* The bank's offshore
hedge funds specializing in mortgage-related
securities collapse. Credit-rating agencies
suddenly downgrade hundreds of subprime
mortgage-backed securities. Banks, securities
firms, hedge funds, mutual funds, and
other investors are left holding suddenly
unmarketable mortgage-backed securities,
whose value plummets.

2008 *Lehman Brothers collapses.* The bank's fall
triggers a U.S. government announcement of a
bailout of major Wall Street banks.

2008 *Bernie Madoff's Ponzi scheme.* Madoff is
arrested for operating a Ponzi scheme, the
largest financial fraud in U.S. history, estimated
to be $64.8 billion.

2008–10 *The Wall Street financial crisis.* Over nine
million homeowners lose their homes to
foreclosure. Almost nine million Americans
lose their jobs. Yet not a single major bank
executive goes to jail or is even indicted.
CEOs of the largest Wall Street banks award
themselves huge bonuses.

2009–17 *Travis Kalanick.* In a quest to build
Uber into the world's dominant ride-hailing
entity, founder and CEO Kalanick flouts

transportation and safety regulations; capitalizes on legal loopholes and gray areas to gain a business advantage over competitors; and promotes and protects top performers even when they verbally and sometimes sexually abuse employees; poaches self-driving-car technology from Google; uses software to evade law enforcement; violates the privacy of riders; and uses predatory tactics on competitors. Kalanick is finally fired by the company's board.

2010 *Deepwater Horizon oil spill.* BP's rig explodes and spills oil into the Gulf of Mexico, the worst oil spill in history.

2012 *Samson scandal.* United Airlines reinstates a money-losing air route between Newark Liberty International Airport and Columbia, South Carolina, at the behest of David Samson, chairman of the Port Authority of New York and New Jersey, who has sway over the Newark airport and has a vacation home near Columbia. United's CEO Jeffery A. Smisek is subsequently fired over the scandal, but receives a severance package totaling $28.6 million.

2013 *Government shutdown.* The federal government is shut down again, for lack of agreement on funding it.

2013 *SAC Capital scandal.* The giant hedge fund pleads guilty to insider trading, paying $1.8 billion in fines, but the fund's founder, Steven A. Cohen, walks away unscathed.

2013 *Bridgegate.* New Jersey officials with ties to Governor Chris Christie close lanes leading to the George Washington Bridge, causing traffic jams apparently designed as political payback against Fort Lee's mayor, Mark Sokolich, who did not support Christie for governor.

2013 *Doping scandal.* After more than a decade of denials, famed cyclist Lance Armstrong confesses to doping.

2013 *Soccer scandal.* As part of a wide-ranging federal investigation into soccer-related improprieties, Chuck Blazer, who had been executive vice president of the United States Soccer Federation, pleads guilty to ten counts of corruption, including racketeering, wire fraud, and money laundering.

2014 *General Motors ignition scandal.* The company recalls nearly thirty million cars worldwide due to faulty ignition switches. The problem was known to GM for at least a decade prior to the recall, but GM had done nothing to remedy it. At least 124 deaths and 275 injuries result.

2015 *Hyperpartisanship soars.* After Republicans gain control of both houses of Congress, Mitch McConnell, the GOP's highest-ranking member of Congress, says his "number one aim" is to unseat Democratic president Barack Obama.

2015 *Martin Shkreli.* The Turing Pharmaceuticals CEO raises the price of a single pill of Daraprim, which treats a parasitic infection that

can be deadly when it afflicts unborn babies
and people with HIV and AIDS, from $13.50
to $750.

2016 *Chicago police scandal.* The Justice Department
finds that the Chicago Police Department has
used excessive force against African American
residents. The report comes two years after the
killing of Laquan McDonald by Chicago police
officer Jason Van Dyke.

2016 *Price-gouging by Mylan Pharmaceuticals.*
The firm ratchets up the price of its EpiPen
emergency injection kit, containing only about
$1 worth of the drug epinephrine, to $609 a
box. Mylan has an effective monopoly on the
lifesaving product. The company's revenue
skyrockets to $11 billion. In 2016, Robert Coury,
Mylan's chairman, receives compensation of
$98 million (including vesting of prior stock
options, $160 million).

2016 *KPMG scandal.* Partners at KPMG, one of
the big four accounting firms, including the
head of its auditing practice, fail to report
leaked information they have received about
inspections planned by its regulator, the Public
Company Accounting Oversight Board, which
was established after the accounting scandals at
Enron. The information has enabled partners to
know in advance which audits will be inspected
so they can make sure any targeted audits are
clean.

2016 *Greg Gianforte scandal.* On the eve of his election to the House of Representatives, Greg Gianforte beats up a reporter who asks him a question he dislikes.

2017 *Baltimore police scandal.* The Justice Department finds that the Baltimore Police Department has systematically abused its power with regard to African American residents. The report comes more than a year after the local police apparently caused the death of Freddie Gray.

2017 *Wells Fargo scandal.* Top executives at Wells Fargo Bank are found to have pushed bank employees to create multiple new accounts for customers who didn't request or want them, and sell them auto insurance they didn't need.

This list is not intended to be a scientific sample. Not every breach on the list is as serious as every other. Some were blatantly illegal, some were abuses of power, others were exploitations of ambiguities in laws, the rest were considered by many to be unethical. All made the list because they shocked many people into saying something like "I didn't know anyone could do that" or "That's just *wrong.*" All were the result of people seeking personal gains in wealth or power at the expense of the common good. All contributed to accumulating cynicism and distrust.

The list doesn't prove that such violations have been on the upswing over the past decades, and it's not as if America was free from wrongdoing before the 1970s. Consider Warren G. Harding's dizzyingly corrupt administration, or the baseball scandal of 1919, when eight members of the Chicago White Sox were accused of intentionally losing the World Series in exchange for money from gamblers. There has been corruption and racism in police departments extending back to the nineteenth century. In the 1950s and 1960s, CEOs reassured the public that DDT, asbestos, tobacco, toxic waste dumps like Love Canal, and automobiles without seat belts were all safe.

What's new is the escalation of it all. No one who has lived through the past five decades can have failed to notice the breakdown. The effect, in the words of the late senator and professor Daniel Patrick Moynihan, has been to "define deviancy down." Conduct previously considered wrong has come to be seen as normal. Trust in every major institution of America has declined. Cynicism prevails.

CHAPTER 5

Three Structural Breakdowns

SOME OF THE SCANDALS and events I've listed changed the rules of the game significantly, from concern for the common good to whatever it takes to win. Three chain reactions in particular bear highlighting. In all three, initial exploitations of trust were rationalized by the exploiters as being necessary and legitimate. Those exploitations were then replicated by others who felt they had no choice but to do the same, or else be at a disadvantage. Over time, each of these practices grew to be so commonplace they became part of the system itself. They made it acceptable to gain wealth or power at the expense of the integrity of the system as a whole.

1 *Nixon's Watergate, Robert Bork's hearing, and whatever-it-takes-to-win politics*

The scandal that came to be known as "Watergate" and led to Richard Nixon's resignation from the presidency was a shock to the American political system. Afterward, analogous to putting locks on the doors, Congress enacted many reforms, but they were eventually watered down or found by the Supreme Court to be unconstitutional. The Watergate scandal began an era of whatever-it-takes-to-win politics.

As Carl Bernstein and Bob Woodward, the *Washington Post* reporters who broke the Watergate story, later wrote, "In his last remarks about Watergate as a senator, 77-year-old Sam Ervin, a revered constitutionalist respected by both parties, posed a final question: 'What was Watergate?' The president and his aides, Ervin answered, 'had a lust for political power.' That lust, he explained, 'blinded them to ethical considerations and legal requirements; to Aristotle's aphorism that the good of man must be the end of politics.' Nixon had lost his moral authority as president. His secret tapes—and what they reveal—will probably be his most lasting legacy. On them, he is heard talking almost endlessly about what would be good for him, his place in history and, above all, his grudges, animosities and schemes for revenge. The dog that never seems to bark is any discussion of what is good and necessary for the well-being of the nation."

The details of what occurred still shock. In 1970, Nixon authorized break-ins or "black bag jobs" of people considered domestic security threats. One early goal was to destroy the reputation of Daniel Ellsberg, who had leaked to the news media the Pentagon Papers, showing that the Johnson administration had lied to the American people about the Vietnam War. Nixon's burglars broke into the office of Ellsberg's psychiatrist, seeking information that might smear Ellsberg and undermine his credibility in the antiwar movement. "You can't drop it, Bob," Nixon told his assistant H. R. Haldeman in June 1971, referring to Ellsberg. "You can't let the Jew steal that stuff and get away with it. You understand?"

In early 1972, Nixon launched a plan for spying on and sabotaging Democrats in the upcoming presidential campaign, including wiretaps and burglaries. His henchmen paid the chauffeur of Senator Ed Muskie, whom Nixon considered his most likely Democratic opponent, to photograph Muskie's internal memos and strategy documents, and paid others to dig up dirt on the sex life of Senator Ted Kennedy, a potential opponent in 1976. "I'd really like to get Kennedy taped," Nixon told Haldeman. They inserted a retired Secret Service agent into the team protecting Kennedy who, Haldeman assured Nixon, would "do anything that I tell him." Nixon replied, "We just might get lucky and catch this son of a bitch and ruin him for '76," adding, "That's going to be fun." Nixon ordered another assistant, John Ehrlichman, to direct the Internal Revenue Service to investigate the tax returns of all likely Democratic presidential candidates, including Kennedy. "Are we going after their tax returns?" Nixon asked. "You know what I mean? There's a lot of gold in them thar hills."

In the early morning of June 17, 1972, a team of burglars wearing business suits and rubber gloves broke into the headquarters of the Democratic National Committee in the Watergate office building in Washington. The burglars were discovered and arrested, and the FBI immediately began an investigation. Six days later, Attorney General John Mitchell proposed to Nixon that he order the CIA to claim national security secrets would be compromised if the FBI didn't halt its investigation. Nixon agreed. "Play it tough," he directed. "That's the way they play it, and that's the way we are going to play it."

Six weeks after the burglars' arrest, according to Woodward and Bernstein, Nixon and Haldeman discussed paying them off to keep them from talking to federal investigators. "They have to be paid," Nixon said. "That's all there is to that." On March 21, 1973, Nixon counsel John W. Dean reported that the burglars were still demanding money. Nixon asked, "How much money do you need?" Dean estimated a million dollars over the following two years. Nixon responded, "You could get it in cash, and I know where it could be gotten." They discussed using a secret stash hidden in the White House, laundering the money through bookmakers, and empaneling a grand jury so the burglars could plead the Fifth Amendment or claim memory failure. Nixon praised Dean's efforts. "You handled it just right. You contained it. Now after the election, we've got to have another plan." Four days after the tapes revealing much of this malfeasance were released, on August 9, 1974, Nixon was forced to resign.

I relate these details to remind you just how far Nixon went in violating the norms of the modern presidency in order to retain power. Even though his actions led to his resignation and to many reforms, Americans' trust in politics was deeply shaken. Public outrage continued when Nixon's successor, Gerald Ford, granted him a full pardon. Ford believed the nation had to be shielded from the pain and disruption of a president put on criminal trial and possibly imprisoned. Yet to many Americans, the fact that Nixon would not be held accountable felt like another assault on the common good. To make matters worse, Nixon continued to insist he had not participated in any crimes. Woodward and Bernstein note that in his 1977 television interviews with British journalist David Frost, Nixon conceded he had "let the American people down" but refused to admit to any illegality. "I didn't think of it as a cover-up. I didn't intend a cover-up. Let me say, if I intended the cover-up, believe me, I would have done it." Nixon added, "If the president does it, that means it is not illegal."

The ripples from Nixon's disregard of the common good can still be felt today.

To my mind, the next major incident of whatever-it-takes-to-win politics occurred in 1987, with the Senate hearing on Ronald Reagan's nominee for the Supreme Court, Robert Bork. I had worked for Bork in the late 1970s when he was solicitor general under President Gerald Ford. I disagreed with him on many matters but always found him to be a man of keen intelligence and integrity. When Reagan nominated him, I worried about Bork's conservative leanings but I had no doubt he would be a thoughtful jurist who would carefully consider the common good.

I was surprised when liberal groups fought Bork's nomination in ways that previously had been thought unacceptable: mass mailings and advertisements that disparaged him; unfounded claims that Bork's wife, a former Roman Catholic nun, would influence his decisions on abortion; leaks to the press of lists of videos Bork had rented from a local video store (ultimately revealing nothing of interest); charges that with Bork on the Court "women would be forced into back-alley abortions, blacks would sit at segregated lunch counters, rogue police could break down citizens' doors in midnight raids." It was scorched-earth ideological warfare so personal and mean-spirited that it generated a new verb: "to Bork," meaning to systematically defame and vilify someone in public life. No holds were barred. The process we previously had come to expect for considering Supreme Court nominees—respectful deliberation, respect for the institutional integrity of the Senate, preservation of comity among senators—was subverted to the goal of winning.

Bork's liberal opponents won the fight, but they opened the way to whatever-it-takes tactics in battles over subsequent Supreme Court nominees, such as the bitter fight over Clarence Thomas's nomination in 1991, which Thomas's backers won. The tactics used on the Bork nomination also legitimized, at least in the minds of Republicans, Senate majority leader Mitch McConnell's refusal in 2016 to hold hearings on Barack Obama's Supreme Court nominee, Merrick Garland, even though Obama had almost ten months left of his presidency. I'm sure the liberals who opposed Bork thought they were acting for the common good. But their tactics were another broken window, inviting more whatever-it-takes tactics in American politics. From then on, there was little to restrain partisanship.

When Newt Gingrich took over the House at the start of 1995, he brought whatever-it-takes politics to a new extreme. I was secretary of labor then, and I remember the sharp change in barometric pressure when Gingrich took the helm, as if a hurricane had blown in. Before that time, when I'd testified on the Hill, I had come in for tough questioning from Republican senators and representatives, which was their job. After January 1995, I was verbally assaulted. Almost overnight, the Labor Department was deluged with demands from new Republican House chairmen for documents and information about all sorts of mundane things. I knew they were fishing expeditions intended to find any small error or omission that might be used to catch me, and then fry me. Washington was transformed from a place where legislators sought common ground into a war zone. Compromise was replaced by brinkmanship, bargaining by obstruction, normal legislative maneuvering by threats to close down government—which occurred at the end of 1995, a prelude to another shutdown in 2013 over raising the debt ceiling. Two years later, Gingrich and his stop-at-nothing colleagues voted to impeach Bill Clinton. According to Norman Ornstein and Thomas Mann, two respected and nonpartisan political observers, "The forces Mr. Gingrich unleashed destroyed whatever comity existed across party lines."

.　　　.　　　.

Whatever-it-takes partisanship continued to escalate on both sides. Before the presidential election of 2008, both John McCain, the Republican candidate, and Barack Obama accepted limits on campaign contributions in exchange for public financing. When Obama's powerful fund-raising ability became apparent, however, he abandoned his commitment. During the first two years of his presidency, when Democrats controlled both houses of Congress, Obama was able to enact legislation without any Republican input or cooperation. In 2010 Democrats enacted the Affordable Care Act without a single Republican vote. Not surprisingly, after Republicans assumed control of the House in January 2011 and the Senate in January 2015, they escalated whatever-it-takes partisanship— obstructing nearly everything Obama wanted to do—and sought to repeal the Affordable Care Act.

Republican obstructionism caused Obama to escalate further, announcing at his first cabinet meeting after Democrats lost control of the Senate that "we're not just going to be waiting for legislation. . . . I've got a pen and I've got a phone. And I can use that pen to sign executive orders and take executive actions and administrative actions that move the ball forward." When Obama couldn't pass legislation providing amnesty for certain categories of undocumented immigrants, he did it by executive order. Rather than try to enact stronger environmental protections, he used regulations under the Clean Air Act. He employed executive actions to close Guantánamo Bay, join the Paris Accord on climate change, allow transgender students to use public bathrooms that do not match their biological gender, and move toward stricter gun control and stronger financial regulation.

Liberals might say that by circumventing the Republican roadblock Obama achieved the common good. At the same time, though, he also undermined a larger common good—the constitutional system of separation of powers and of democratic deliberation. One might legitimately ask, What other options did he have at this point? Nonetheless, the gains he managed to achieve would prove short-lived. And, without those rudders, public policy would thereafter swing wildly from one extreme to the other: When Republicans regained control of both Congress and the presidency in 2016, they had no incentive to fix defects in the Affordable Care Act. They spent months instead trying to repeal it. As president, Donald Trump revoked or reversed many of Obama's executive actions, through executive orders of his own.

Trump escalated conflict to another level. He used white resentment against the nation's growing population of blacks, Latinos, and immigrants to solidify his largely white, working-class base—urging travel bans on Muslims, immigration enforcement raids on Latino communities, photo IDs to vote, a wall along the Mexican border, the purging of voter registration lists, and bans on transgender personnel in the military. These measures had nothing whatever to do with the central problems facing the nation nor with the deep unease at economic exclusion and vulnerability much of his core base experienced. They served only to advance a narrow political agenda at the expense of the common good.

In all these respects, the common good has been subordinated to winning. Step by step, our system of government has been sacrificed to the goal of short-term political success. The cumulative cost to trustworthiness and integrity of our democratic institutions has been incalculable.

2 *Michael Milken, Jack Welch, and whatever it takes
to maximize profits*

A second chain reaction that undermined the common good was set off in the 1980s as "corporate raiders" mounted hostile takeovers of corporations, financed by risky bonds. The raiders made fortunes, Wall Street became the most powerful force in the economy, and CEOs began to devote themselves entirely and obsessively to maximizing the short-term value of shares of stock. The new rule was: Do whatever it takes to make huge profits.

Before then it was assumed that large corporations had responsibilities to all their "stakeholders"—not just their shareholders but also their workers, the towns and cities where their headquarters and facilities were located, and the nation. "The job of management," proclaimed Frank Abrams, chairman of Standard Oil of New Jersey, in a 1951 address, "is to maintain an equitable and working balance among the claims of the various directly affected interest groups ... stockholders, employees, customers, and the public at large." In November 1956, *Time* magazine noted that business leaders were willing to "judge their actions, not only from the standpoint of profit and loss but of profit and loss to the community." CEOs had become "corporate statesmen," responsible for the common good of the nation. General Electric, the magazine said, sought to serve the "balanced best interests" of all its stakeholders. As paper executive J. D. Zellerbach told *Time*, Americans "regard business management as a stewardship, and they expect it to operate the economy as a public trust for the benefit of all the people." These sentiments may seem quaint today, but they laid the basis for rapid economic growth and, with strong unions, an equally rapid expansion of the middle class.

Starting in the 1980s, though, as a result of the corporate takeovers mounted by raiders such as Michael Milken—who is credited with inventing the use of high risk "junk" bonds for such raids—as well as Ivan Boesky and Carl Icahn, a wholly different understanding about the purpose of the corporation emerged. The raiders targeted companies that could deliver higher returns to their shareholders if they abandoned their other stakeholders— fighting unions, cutting the pay of workers or firing them, automating as many jobs as possible, and abandoning their original communities by shuttering factories and moving jobs to a state with lower labor costs, or moving them abroad.

The raiders pushed shareholders to vote out directors who wouldn't make these sorts of changes and vote in directors who would (or else sell their shares to the raiders, who'd do the dirty work). During the whole of the 1970s there were only 13 hostile takeovers of big companies valued at $1 billion or more. During the 1980s, there were 150. Between 1979 and 1989, financial entrepreneurs mounted more than two thousand leveraged buyouts, in which they bought out shareholders with borrowed money, each buyout exceeding $250 million. As a result, CEOs across America, facing the possibility of being replaced by a CEO who would maximize shareholder value, began to view their responsibilities differently. Few events change minds more profoundly than the imminent possibility of being sacked. As a result, the corporate statesmen of previous decades became the corporate butchers of the 1980s and 1990s, whose nearly exclusive focus was—in the meat-ax parlance that suddenly became fashionable—to "cut out the fat," "cut to the bone," and make their companies "lean and mean." Given what was to follow, it's enough to make one a vegan.

Between 1981, when Jack Welch took the helm at GE, and 2001, when he retired, the firm's stock value catapulted from $14 billion to $400 billion. Welch accomplished this largely by slashing American jobs. Before he became CEO, most GE employees had spent their entire careers with the company, typically at one of its facilities in upstate New York. But between 1981 and 1985, a quarter of them—one hundred thousand in all—lost their jobs, earning Welch the moniker "Neutron Jack," and the growing admiration of the business community. Welch encouraged his senior managers to replace 10 percent of their subordinates every year in order to keep GE competitive. As GE opened facilities abroad, staffed by foreign workers costing a small fraction of what GE had paid its American employees, the corporation all but abandoned upstate New York. Between the mid-1980s and the late 1990s, GE slashed its American workforce by half (to about 160,000) while nearly doubling its foreign workforce (to 130,000).

Over the years, corporate raiders have morphed into more respectable "private equity managers" and "activist investors," and hostile takeovers have become rare. That's only because corporate norms have utterly changed. It is now assumed that corporations exist only to maximize shareholder returns. CEOs have become so obsessed by shareholder value that Roberto Goizueta, CEO of Coca-Cola, proclaimed in 1988, "I wrestle with how to build shareholder value from the time I get up in the morning to the time I go to bed. I even think about it when I am shaving." Goizueta's obsession was quite different from the views of his predecessors, such as Coca-Cola's president William Robinson, who in 1959 told an audience at Fordham Law School that executives should *not* put stockholders first. They should "balance" the interests of the stockholder, the community, the customer, and the employee.

Corporations have used their profits to give shareholders dividends and buy back their shares of stock—thereby reducing the number of shares outstanding and giving stock prices short-term boosts. All of this has meant more money for the top executives of big companies, whose pay began to be linked to share prices. CEO pay soared from an average of 20 times that of the typical worker in the 1960s to almost 300 times by 2017.

Are we better off? Some argue shareholder capitalism has proven to be more "efficient" than stakeholder capital- ism. It has moved economic resources to where they're most productive, and thereby enabled the economy to grow faster. By this view, stakeholder capitalism locked up resources in unproductive ways, CEOs were too compla- cent, corporations were too fat—employing workers they didn't need, and paying them too much—and they were too tied to their communities.

It is a tempting argument, but in hindsight a fallacious one. Any change that allows some people to become bet- ter off without causing others to be worse off is technically a more "efficient" use of resources. But when all or most of these efficiency gains go to a few people at the top—as has been the case since the 1980s—the common good is not necessarily improved. Just look at the flat or declining wages of most Americans, their growing economic inse- curity, and the abandoned communities now littering the nation. Then look at the record corporate profits, soaring CEO pay, and jaw-dropping compensation on Wall Street. All Americans are stakeholders in the American economy, and most stakeholders have not done well.

As a practical matter, shareholders are not the only parties who invest in corporations and bear some of the risk that the value of their investments might drop. Workers who have been with a firm for years often develop skills and knowledge unique to it. Others may have moved their families to take a job with the firm, buying homes in the community. The community itself may have invested in roads and other infrastructure to accommodate the corporation. When a firm abandons those workers and those communities, these stakeholders lose the value of their investments. Why should no account be taken of their stakes?

Executives claim they have a "fiduciary obligation" to maximize investors' returns. The argument is tautological. It assumes that investors are the only people worthy of consideration. What about the common good? Jared Kushner's real estate company uses arrest warrants to collect debts owed by low-income tenants, often tacking on thousands of dollars in legal fees, because of its "fiduciary obligation" to investors—the largest of which are Jared Kushner and his family. After the company sued one of its tenants for moving out of her apartment without giving the company two months' notice (despite her having done so), the company won an almost $5,000 judgment against her, and then garnished her wages as a home health worker and her bank account. When asked to justify such tactics, the Kushner Companies' chief financial officer told *The New York Times* that the company had a "fiduciary obligation" to collect as much revenue as possible. One means of making sure tenants paid their rent on time and did not break their leases early was to instill in them a sense of fear about violating a lease.

The goal of maximizing profits has leached into sectors of the economy that had once been based on the common good, such as health care. A century ago, hospitals and health insurers had palpable public responsibilities. The original purpose of health insurance plans, devised in the 1920s at the Baylor University Medical Center in Dallas, was not to generate profits. It was to cover as many people as possible. The nonprofits Blue Cross and Blue Shield accepted everyone who wanted to become a member, and all members paid the same rate regardless of age or health. By the 1960s, Blue Cross was providing hospital coverage to more than fifty million Americans.

In the 1970s and 1980s, though, some entrepreneurs saw ways to make big money by exploiting this common good. They founded for-profit insurance companies like Aetna and Cigna that, unhampered by the Blues' charitable mission, accepted only younger and healthier patients. This reduced their costs, enabling them to charge lower premiums than the Blues while still pocketing big profits. The Blues couldn't possibly compete. So in 1994, Blue Cross and Blue Shield succumbed and became for-profits— marking the end of nonprofit health insurance—turning the American health care system into one that eagerly insured healthy people while trying to avoid sick people, or charging people with chronic health problems a fortune for coverage.

Big financial houses, meanwhile, went from small privately held investment banks to giant corporations whose shares were traded on stock exchanges. This has also had unfortunate consequences. When investment bankers made all the profits and also suffered all the losses from their bets, they tended to be cautious. In order to understand the risks they were taking on, partners kept their banks small and their transactions relatively simple. But by 2000, because of deregulation, Wall Street had morphed into megabanks with employees numbering in the hundreds of thousands, and spanning the globe. There were no longer any constraints on risky bets. Shareholders bore the costs while those who made the bets got many of the upside gains in the form of giant bonuses. Bankers had every incentive to grab the cheapest funding possible to make the riskiest possible bets, and that led to the crash of 2008.

When the only purpose of business is to make as much money as possible in the shortest time frame, regardless of how it's done, the common good is easily sacrificed. In pursuit of high profits, whatever it takes, CEOs and the corporations they run have ignored or circumvented the intent of laws to protect workers, communities, the environment, and consumers. They abandoned the principle of equal economic opportunity that underlay their obligations to all stakeholders, and have too often put themselves first. Despite his avowed goal to rebuild customer confidence in Wells Fargo, John Stumpf didn't care about his customers; he apparently cared only about himself. Although Martin Shkreli said he was motivated by investors who "expect me to maximize profits . . . to 100 percent of the profit curve," it turned out his real motive was Martin Shkreli.

3   *Lewis Powell's memo, Tony Coelho's bargain, Wall Street's bailout, and whatever it takes to rig the economy*

The third chain reaction eroding the common good came as a consequence of the first two. Whatever-it-takes politics removed all constraints on gaining and keeping political power. Whatever it takes to make big money eliminated all checks on unbridled greed. Put them together and what did we get? We got money pouring into politics in order to change the rules of the game in favor of big corporations and the wealthy, so they could rake in even more.

The start of this can be traced to 1971, when future Supreme Court justice Lewis Powell argued in a memo he wrote at the request of the U.S. Chamber of Commerce that the "American economic system is under broad attack" from consumer, labor, and environmental groups. In reality, these groups were doing nothing more than enforcing the implicit social contract I've referred to, ensuring that corporations were responsible to all their stakeholders. But Powell and the Chamber saw it differently. Powell urged businesses to mobilize for political combat. "Business must learn the lesson . . . that political power is necessary; that such power must be assiduously cultivated; and that when necessary, it must be used aggressively and with determination—without embarrassment and without the reluctance which has been so characteristic of American business." Powell stressed that the critical ingredients for success were organization and funding: "Strength lies in . . . the scale of financing available only through joint effort, and in the political power available only through united action and national organizations."

Powell's memo unleashed corporate money into politics, growing into the largest force in Washington and most state capitals. Once a few large corporations ramped up their lobbying and campaign contributions, competitors felt they had to do the same or lose out. The number of corporations with public affairs offices in Washington ballooned from one hundred in 1968 to over five hundred a decade later. In 1971, only 175 firms had registered lobbyists in the nation's capital. By 1982, nearly 2,500 had them. The number of corporate Political Action Committees mushroomed from under 300 in 1976 to over 1,200 by 1980. Smaller businesses joined together in trade associations and business groups to do their bidding. Between 1974 and 1980, the Chamber of Commerce doubled its membership. By the 1990s, when I was secretary of labor, corporations employed some 61,000 people to lobby for them, including registered lobbyists and lawyers. That came to more than

100 for each member of Congress. Corporate money has also supported platoons of lawyers who represent corporations and the very rich in regulatory and court proceedings, often outgunning the Justice Department and state attorneys general. Corporations have also funded think tanks and public relations firms.

Most important, corporations began inundating politicians with money for their campaigns. Between the late 1970s and the late 1980s, corporate Political Action Committees increased their expenditures on congressional races nearly fivefold. Labor union PAC spending rose only about half as fast. By the 2016 campaign cycle, corporations and Wall Street contributed $34 for every $1 donated by labor unions and all public interest organizations combined. Wealthy individuals also accounted for a growing share. In 1980, the richest one-hundredth of 1 percent of Americans provided 10 percent of contributions to federal elections. By 2012, they provided 40 percent. The Supreme Court has made all this worse through a series of decisions holding that money is speech under the First Amendment and corporations are people.

Both political parties have transformed themselves from mainly state and local organizations that channeled the views of members upward, into giant top-down fundraising machines. In the 1980s, the Democratic Party began drinking at the same trough as the GOP. "Business has to deal with us whether they like it or not, because we're the majority," crowed Democratic representative Tony Coelho, who, as head of the Democratic Congressional Campaign Committee, commenced a shakedown of corporate America. Coelho's Democrats soon achieved a rough parity with Republicans in contributions from corporate and Wall Street campaign coffers. It proved a Faustian bargain. Once hooked on corporate money, Democrats couldn't unhook themselves. The Democrats' dependence on big corporations became evident when, months before the party's trouncing in the 1994 midterms, many congressional Democrats voted against Bill Clinton's health care plan because their corporate sponsors opposed it.

Business executives haven't cared which party they contribute to as long as the money gets results. During the 2016 Republican primaries, Donald Trump, who was then getting attacked by his GOP rivals for having once donated money to Hillary Clinton, explained that "as a businessman and a very substantial donor to very important people, when you give, they do whatever the hell you want them to do. As a businessman, I need that." Apparently, he got what he needed. After Trump's charitable foundation made a $25,000 contribution to a campaign organization linked to Florida's attorney general, she decided not to open a fraud investigation of Trump University that her office had been considering.

Businesses have also dangled before public officials the lure of well-paying jobs after government. In the 1970s only about 3 percent of retiring members of Congress went on to become Washington lobbyists. By 2016, fully half of all retiring senators and 42 percent of retiring representatives had turned to lobbying, regardless of party affiliation.

This wasn't because more recent retirees have had fewer qualms than their predecessors about making money off their contacts in government. It was because the financial rewards from corporate lobbying had ballooned. The revolving door rotates the other way, too: If a lobbyist can land a plum job in an administration, he or she becomes even more valuable on leaving. In his first six months as president, Trump handed control of every major regulatory agency to lobbyists from the industries they would oversee.

The *quid* is tightly linked to the *quo*. After Wall Street became a gusher of campaign funds starting in the 1980s, the Street got Congress to repeal Depression-era regulations that for a half century had prevented another great crash—restrictions on interstate banking, on intermingling investment and commercial banking, and on banks becoming publicly held corporations. This freed the Street to once again gamble with other people's money, and led in 2008 to a financial crisis similar to the one that occurred in 1929. A giant taxpayer-funded bailout kept the big banks from going under and avoided another Great Depression, but homeowners and workers caught in the downdraft received no such help. Millions lost their jobs, homes, and savings. Millions more felt vulnerable.

Not surprisingly, the day-to-day decisions emanating from Congress and the White House no longer reflect the views of average Americans. After examining 1,799 policy issues in detail, two eminent researchers, Princeton professor Martin Gilens and Professor Benjamin Page of

Northwestern University, concluded that "the preferences of the average American appear to have only a minuscule, near-zero, statistically non-significant impact upon public policy."

All of this has enhanced the economic gains flowing to big firms and the wealthy, while reducing the share going to the majority of Americans. It's been a vast redistribution, essentially taking money out of the paychecks of the middle class and poor, and channeling it upward. Intellectual property rights—patents, trademarks, and copyrights—have been enlarged and extended, allowing pharmaceuticals, high-tech, biotechnology, and many entertainment companies to preserve their monopolies longer. This has meant higher prices for average consumers, including the highest pharmaceutical costs of any advanced nation. At the same time, antitrust laws have been relaxed, resulting in large profits for firms like Monsanto, which sets the prices for most of the nation's seed corn; for a handful of high-tech companies with market power over network portals and platforms (Amazon, Facebook, Apple, and Google); cable companies with little or no broadband competition (Comcast, AT&T, Verizon); and the largest Wall Street banks, among others. As with the broadening of intellectual property rights, the relaxing of antitrust laws has raised prices and reduced services for average Americans. We have the most expensive and slowest broadband of any industrialized nation, for example. In 2016, *The Economist* magazine reported that two-thirds of all corporate sectors have become more concentrated since the 1990s, making corporations far more profitable than at any time since the 1920s.

Contract laws have been altered so that consumers and employees can't take their grievances to court; they have to use arbitrators selected by big corporations. A few states have enacted "noncompete" laws making it impossible for employees to leave their jobs for new ones unless they can show that the move wouldn't "adversely affect" their current employer—leaving workers and their wages at the mercy of their bosses. Securities laws have been relaxed to allow insider trading of confidential information, and to let CEOs use stock buybacks to boost share prices when they cash in their own stock options. Tax laws have been altered to create loopholes for the partners of hedge funds and private equity funds, special favors for the oil and gas industry, lower marginal income tax rates on the highest incomes, and reduced estate taxes on great wealth.

Bankruptcy laws have been loosened for large corporations—notably airlines and automobile manufacturers—allowing them to rip up labor contracts, threaten closures unless they receive wage concessions, and leave workers and communities stranded. Notably, bankruptcy has not been extended to homeowners who owe more on their homes than the homes are worth, or to graduates over-burdened with student debt. Meanwhile, as I've noted, the largest banks and auto manufacturers were bailed out in the downturn of 2008–09. The result has been to shift the risks of economic failure onto the backs of average working people and taxpayers.

Finally, taxes have been reduced on corporations and the wealthy, even as corporate profits and the incomes of the rich have soared.

In all these ways, and more, the market has been altered to redistribute money from the middle class and poor to the wealthy. It is a vicious cycle. As large corporations and the wealthy accumulate more of the nation's assets, they gain more power to rig the market to their advantage.

CHAPTER 6

The Decline
of the Good in Common

TO REPEAT, three exploitations of trust set off chain reactions that have undermined the common good: *Whatever-it-takes-to-win politics* disregarded what had been the unwritten rules of good government, based on equal political rights—enabling the most powerful players to extract all political gains. *Whatever it takes to maximize profits* rejected what had been the unwritten rules of corporate responsibility, based on obligations to all stakeholders—allowing CEOs, Wall Street, and investors to extract all financial gains. *Whatever it takes to rig the economy* dismissed what had been the unwritten rule that the "free market" should work for everyone—permitting the most powerful economic actors to extract almost all economic gains. As a result, the key political and economic institutions of our society—political parties, corporations, and the free market—have abandoned their commitment to the common good.

The consequence has been a catastrophe for most

Americans. By 2016, the typical American household had a net worth 14 percent lower than the typical household in 1984, while the richest one-tenth of 1 percent owned almost as much wealth as the bottom 90 percent put together. Income has become almost as unequal as wealth: Between 1972 and 2016 the pay of the typical American worker dropped 2 percent, adjusted for inflation, although the American economy nearly doubled in size. Most of the income gains went to the top. In 2016, the annual Wall Street bonus pool alone was larger than the annual year-round earnings of all 3.3 million Americans working full-time at the federal minimum wage of $7.25 an hour.

The middle class is shrinking. Whereas 90 percent of American adults born in the early 1940s were earning more than their parents by the time they reached their prime earning years, this proportion has steadily declined; only half of adults born in the mid-1980s are earning more than their parents by their prime earning years.

Most Americans are working longer hours than they had worked decades before and taking fewer sick days or vacations, and they are falling behind the economic security enjoyed by their parents. Nearly one out of every five is in a part-time job. Two-thirds are living paycheck to paycheck. Along with pay, employment benefits have been shriveling. The gap in life expectancy between the nation's most affluent and everyone else is widening as well. Increasing numbers of working Americans have been succumbing to opioids. Death rates have been rising for Americans with high school degrees or less, due to suicides, chronic liver cirrhosis, and poisonings, including drug overdoses.

Discrimination based on race, gender, and ethnicity has magnified these economic differences, and the economic stresses have fueled further bigotry. Many Americans who for decades have been on a downward economic escalator have become easy prey for demagogues peddling the politics of hate. While in the 1950s and 1960s the nation began struggling to overcome racial discrimination, progress has slowed and in many respects reversed. By 2017, a higher share of America's population was in jail or prison than in almost any other country on the planet, and the inmates were disproportionately black and Latino.

The standard explanation for why America has become so economically lopsided is that most Americans are no longer "worth" as much as they were before digital technologies and globalization, and therefore must now settle for lower wages and less security. If they want better jobs, they need more education and better skills.

This account doesn't explain why other advanced economies facing similar forces haven't succumbed to them nearly as dramatically as has the United States. Or why America's U-turn from broadly shared prosperity to stagnant wages for most and great riches for a few occurred so quickly in the late 1970s and 1980s. It doesn't clarify why the pay of top executives at big companies rose so dramatically since then, or why the denizens of Wall Street are now paid tens or hundreds of millions annually.

Nor can it account for the decline in wages of recent college graduates. Although young people with college degrees have continued to outpace people without them, the real average hourly wages of young college graduates have dropped since 2000. A college education has become a prerequisite for joining the middle class, but it is no longer a sure means for gaining ground once admitted to it.

To attribute all this to the impersonal workings of the "free market" is to be blind to the disproportionate political power of America's economic elites over the rules of the game, and their failure to use that power to deliver rising or even stable incomes and jobs to most of the rest of the nation. It is to ignore the increasing willingness of moneyed interests to rig the system for their own benefit, and their dwindling concern for the common good.

As they gained more wealth and power they could have made a different choice. They could have used their political and economic clout to get better schools for all, comprehensive job retraining, wage insurance, better public transportation, and expanded unemployment insurance. They could have pushed for universal health insurance. They could have paid for all this by accepting, even lobbying for, higher taxes on themselves. They could have strengthened rather than fought off unions, and pushed for laws giving workers more rather than less voice. They could have demanded limits on campaign spending.

They did the reverse: They spent more and more of their ever-expanding wealth to alter the rules of the game to their own advantage. We are now living with the consequences. The ethos of whatever-it-takes-to-win has taken a profound toll. Much of the public no longer believes that the major institutions of America are working for the many; they are vessels for the few.

In 1963 over 60 percent of Americans trusted government to do the right thing all or most of the time; nowadays only 16 percent do. In 1964 more than 60 percent thought government was "run for the benefit of all the people," while just 29 percent said government was "pretty much run by a few big interests looking out for themselves." Nowadays the numbers are almost reversed, with 76 percent believing government is run "by a few big interests" and just 19 percent saying government is run "for the benefit of all."*

There has been a similar decline in trust for corporations. In the early 1960s most Americans said they had a "great deal of confidence" in the nation's major companies, banks, and financial institutions. Now just one in ten has a great deal of confidence in them. Public trust has also plummeted for nonprofits—universities, charities, and religious institutions. Trust in the media has dropped as well (even before Donald Trump's disparagement), as has that for the scientific community.

The decline in trust has not been confined to the United States. A similar erosion has occurred in other advanced nations, and for a similar reason. The political and economic systems that fostered widespread prosperity and

---

* The following graphs are based on polling data from the Gallup organization.

Gallup polls of U.S. adults over the last forty years asked "how much confidence you, yourself, have in each" of the following institutions. The graphs below show the combined percentage of those answering a "great deal" or "quite a lot."

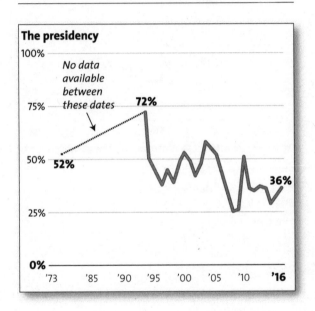

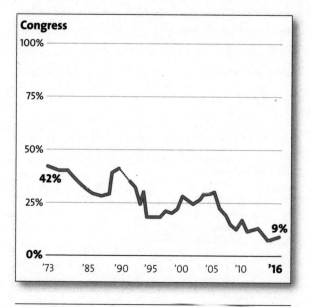

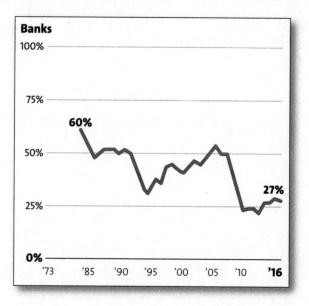

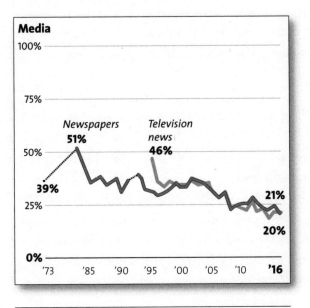

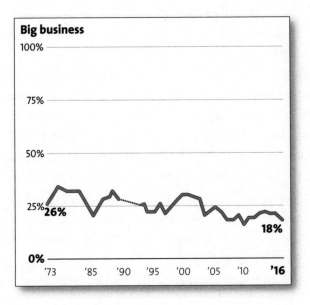

democracy in the three decades after World War II have ceased to work for most people. They became the vehicles for elites to entrench their wealth and power.

When the game is widely seen as rigged in favor of those at the top, others view cheating as acceptable or fear they'll become chumps if they don't cheat. The system becomes rife with smaller bamboozles and con jobs, frauds and swindles. Employees pilfer from employers. Middle managers skim off some of the profits and accept small bribes and kickbacks from contractors. Professional ethics wither among lawyers, doctors, accountants, even professional athletes, who feel freer to cheat. Politicians bestow favors on campaign donors.

As a result, rules are tightened. Time-consuming screening and security checks are imposed. Additional reviews are instituted. Red tape multiplies with the profusion of finagles it seeks to contain. Contracts become longer and more convoluted. There is less willingness to put in extra effort or go the extra mile, to do what is needed but not required, to report unexpected problems or devise new solutions, to blow the whistle on illegality. The overall economy may show some growth because of all this additional spending on security personnel, screeners, accountants, auditors, lawyers, law enforcers, and monitoring equipment, but these defensive expenditures do not enhance anyone's quality of life.

Another consequence is that society shifts from a system of mutual obligations to a system of private deals. Rather than being founded in the common good, political and social relationships increasingly are viewed as contracts. People ask less about their obligations in various situations, more about what's in it for them. When it's all about making deals, one "gets ahead" by getting ahead of others. Duty is replaced by self-aggrandizement and self-promotion. Calls for sacrifice or self-denial are replaced by personal demands for *better* deals.

It is commonly supposed that contemporary Americans are no longer joiners as we once were. We "bowl alone," as sociologist Robert Putnam has put it. Yet this fails to account for a monumental shift in whom we join and for what. We still join together, but now we join for services too expensive to purchase alone—child care, the schools our children attend, recreational facilities, and security. Rather than come together for the common good, we come together to get the best possible deal. We're clustering by income—attracting members who can contribute the most while excluding those who are more costly.

Whether called "private" or "public," the underlying mechanism is the same. Membership dues pay for services in exclusive private residential communities while local property taxes pay for them in exclusive public townships like Vail or Greenwich, but in neither case is the endeavor *common;* it is for people with the same high incomes. Public schools in exclusive communities are "public" in name only because tuition payments are disguised within high home prices, local property taxes, and parental donations. Parents are intent on policing the boundaries, lest a child whose parents haven't paid the same price reap the same advantages as their own child. Hell hath no fury like an upscale parent who thinks another child is getting an unfair advantage by sneaking in under the fence.

In November 2016, school officials in Orinda, California, determined that a seven-year-old named Vivian, whose single mother worked as a live-in nanny for a family in Orinda, did not "reside" in the district and should not be allowed to attend the elementary school she was already attending there. Vivian is Latina and poor, and Orinda is white and wealthy. Orinda's schools are among the best in California—public schools that glean extra revenues from a local parcel tax (that required a two-thirds vote to pass) and parental contributions to the Educational Foundation of Orinda, which "suggests" donations of $600 per child. Harold Freiman, Orinda's district attorney, said the district had to "preserve the resources of the district for all the students." That is, all of Orinda's students. Which is why the district spends some of its dollars to root out children like Vivian. (After Vivian's story exploded in the media, Orinda's school district backed down and informed her mother that Vivian would not be kicked out.)

Private homeowner associations have spearheaded "citizens' movements" against state and local taxes because their members see no reason why they should pay to support families outside the gates when members get everything they need inside, through their dues. As a result, poorer children are increasingly bunched together with other poorer children, within schools that have relatively few resources to begin with. The economic secession of upper-middle-class and wealthy families is also leading America back toward racially segregated neighborhoods and classrooms. The probability that a black student will have white classmates has dropped to what it was before 1954, when the Supreme Court in *Brown v. Board of Education* declared separate schools inherently unequal.

The same mechanism explains the upsurge of private "parents' foundations" in the wake of court decisions requiring richer school districts to subsidize poorer ones. Rather than pay the extra taxes, upscale parents have quietly shifted their support to these charities so they can keep more of their money in the schools their kids attend. Residents of Malibu, California—more solidly affluent than the residents of neighboring Santa Monica, which shares the same school district—want to keep their donations in Malibu schools. Craig Foster, a Malibu resident and former managing director at Morgan Stanley and Credit Suisse, told *The New York Times* that parents who donate their money deserve to benefit from the fruits of their donations. A parent should have "the opportunity to put your money where your heart is," he said. "It has to be an emotional appeal, and it has to be for the benefit of the donor." Benefit of the donor? What happened to the common good?

The extreme economic rewards available to those who

make it compared to the economic perils facing those who don't have caused many parents to become hyper-competitive. They worry that if they don't get their children into good preschools that lead to good primary and secondary schools, and then into good colleges, their offspring will fall backward economically or, alternatively, lose their chance to become well-off. So they're less generous when it comes to sending their tax dollars and donations to schools and children from lower economic classes. As these parents become increasingly efficient at passing their economic status on to their children, they create an ever more rigid class division in America.

Rather than see this for what it is—economic winners seceding from the common good—some commentators condemn the losers for lacking initiative. In his 2012 book *Coming Apart,* sociologist Charles Murray, the darling of conservative intellectuals, attributed the demise of America's white working class to what Murray described as their loss of traditional values of diligence and hard work. He argued they brought their problems on themselves by becoming addicted to drugs, failing to marry, giving birth out of wedlock, dropping out of high school, and remaining jobless for long periods of time. Government has aided and abetted their decline, he argued, by providing help that encourages these social pathologies.

Murray and others of his stripe seem not to have noticed that, as I've said, the wages of the white working class have stagnated or declined for the past forty years, steady jobs once available to them have disappeared, the economic base of their communities has deteriorated, and their share of the nation's income and wealth has dramatically shrunk. It seems far more likely that *these* are the underlying source of the social pathologies Murray chronicles, and that the drug addiction, out-of-wedlock births, lack of education, and unemployment are its symptoms rather than the other way around. This logic is inconvenient, however, because it suggests that any real solution requires reversing the widening inequities that have hit the old working class especially hard, and embracing a more inclusive view of the common good.

Many commentators embrace a kind of social Darwinism in which struggling whites, like poor blacks, are assumed to be unfit to survive. During the 2016 Republican presidential primaries, *National Review* columnist Kevin Williamson wrote that "these dysfunctional, downscale communities . . . deserve to die. Economically, they are negative assets. Morally, they are indefensible. Forget all your cheap theatrical Bruce Springsteen crap. Forget your sanctimony about struggling Rust Belt factory towns. . . . The white American underclass is in thrall to a vicious, selfish culture whose main products are misery and used heroin needles. Donald Trump's speeches make them feel good. So does OxyContin." In a similar vein, during the congressional fight over repealing the Affordable Care Act in the spring of 2017, Alabama congressman Mo Brooks argued that repeal would reduce "the cost to those people who lead good lives. They're healthy, they've done the things to keep their bodies healthy." Mick Mulvaney,

Trump's budget director, conceded that while people who "get cancer" should have some sort of safety net, he was quick to add "that doesn't mean we should take care of the person who sits at home, eats poorly, and gets diabetes."

America's political and economic leaders paid little heed when, in the years leading up to the financial crisis of 2008, highly paid bankers pocketed huge sums while exposing most Americans to extraordinary economic risks. The people who subsequently lost their jobs, savings, and homes, though, were understandably outraged—especially when these same bankers suffered no consequences. Within a few years of the financial crisis, most of the bankers returned to pocketing vast fortunes, but most other Americans were still living with the consequences. Their anger began to engulf American politics on both sides of the aisle. In the 2016 Democratic primaries, Bernie Sanders said, "This type of rigged economy is not what America is supposed to be about." At the start of her campaign, Hillary Clinton conceded that the "deck is still stacked in favor of those at the top." Candidate Donald Trump proclaimed, "The system is rigged against the citizens," and that he was the only candidate "who cannot be bought"—a refrain he repeated all the way to the White House.

The left has focused its ire on corporations and Wall Street; the right, on government. In fact the two were—are—inextricably related. Trump's antiestablishment authoritarian populism overlapped with Sanders's antiestablishment democratic populism in condemning elites that made off with almost all the gains. "The establishment protected itself, but not the citizens of our country. Their victories have not been your victories; their triumphs have not been your triumphs; and while they celebrated in our nation's Capital, there was little to celebrate for struggling families all across our land," said Trump in his inaugural speech.

Some individuals, like Martin Shkreli and others I've mentioned, have directly abused the public's trust. Most of America's political and economic elites—in Washington's corridors of power, within the executive suites of large corporations, and on Wall Street—have been guilty of simply playing along. They have averted their eyes from the disintegration of the common good. They have failed to insist on major reforms. They have denied, rationalized, and told themselves the disintegration was inevitable.

Yet the arbitrariness and unfairness is widely felt. In a 2001 Gallup poll, 76 percent of Americans were satisfied with opportunities to get ahead by working hard, and only 22 percent were dissatisfied. By 2014, only 54 percent were satisfied, with 45 percent dissatisfied. According to the Pew Research Center, the percentage of Americans who felt that most people who want to get ahead could do so through hard work dropped by 14 points between 2000 and 2014.

Aristotle warned that excessive inequality can bring political instability. You can see and feel the anger even in mundane situations. As first-class sections of airplanes have become more spacious, they seem to be triggering more incidents of air rage among passengers seated in the back. Researchers Katherine DeCelles of the University of Toronto and Michael Norton of Harvard Business School analyzed "disruptive passenger incidents" in an airline's database of millions of domestic and international airline flights. They found that flights with a first-class section were nearly four times more likely to have incidents of "belligerent behavior" or "emotional outbursts" in their economy class. Such incidents were even more likely when economy passengers had to walk through the first-class section to get to their seats than when they entered through the middle of the plane and bypassed the first-class section.

This sort of anger can attach itself to any convenient scapegoat—to immigrants, foreigners, Latinos, African Americans, women, particular religious groups, opposing political parties. It's an open invitation to demagogues to sow division as a political tactic, and build political power based on bigotry and resentment. As I've noted, democracies require sufficient social cohesion that citizens regard the interests and views of those with whom they disagree as being worthy of equal consideration to their own. Unfortunately, the percentage of Americans who regard the other party as a fundamental threat has been growing steadily. By 2014—before the acrimony of the 2016 presidential campaign and the divisiveness of the Trump presidency—35 percent of Republicans saw the Democratic Party as a "threat to the nation's well-being" and 27 percent of Democrats regarded Republicans the same way, according to Pew.

Under these circumstances, people can become suscep-
tible to demagogues who tell them not to believe researchers, scientists, journalists, and other fact-finders who don't
support the demagogues' views. As a result, truth itself
is imperiled as a common good. Republican senator Jeff
Flake wrote of the 2016 electorate, "Who could blame the
people who felt abandoned and ignored by the major parties for reaching in despair for a candidate who offered
oversimplified answers to infinitely complex questions
and managed to entertain them in the process? With hindsight, it is clear that we all but ensured the rise of Donald
Trump."

Can we restore the common good? Can the system be
made to work for the good of all?

PART III

Can the Common Good

Be Restored?

CHAPTER 7

Leadership as Trusteeship

WHAT CHOICE DO WE HAVE other than to try to restore a commitment to the common good? Without it, we are no longer a functioning society. Yet given the serious depletion of the pool of trust on which our society depends, reversing the whatever-it-takes forces that have eroded the common good during the past half century poses a daunting challenge. They can't be reversed through better laws or wiser policies, because in order to make such laws and policies there must first be a strong consensus that they're necessary, as well as the political power to get them enacted and to enforce them in ways they cannot be circumvented. No such consensus exists and no such power is readily available. So we have to go deeper, back to the attitudes and understandings that shape public morality, in the hopes of possibly strengthening them.

One place to begin is with leadership. I'm talking about people vested with formal authority to run major businesses, government, universities, charities, unions, and faith-based institutions. All of them carry around in their heads a definition of what it means to be successful. These days that definition is usually focused on accumulating for themselves and their organizations more power or wealth—whatever it takes. But this definition is profoundly inadequate. Leaders must see that part of their responsibility is to rebuild public trust in the institutions they oversee.

Leadership must entail trusteeship. Leaders are stewards of the unwritten rules we once took for granted, that constituted the common good. As I've shown, CEOs half a century ago understood that corporations were not just for shareholders but also for employees, communities, customers, and the public as a whole. Banks existed not to make wild bets with other people's money but to protect depositors' and investors' savings and to prudently lend them. Health insurers existed to provide coverage to everyone who needed it, not to make big money by cherry-picking the healthiest. Political parties existed to organize and inform voters, not to corrupt our democracy with giant campaign contributions and negative ads. Over time, these institutions and their leaders seem to have forgotten that their legitimacy depends on them advancing the common good, and that leadership is a public trust.

Trusteeship should be baked into our understanding of successful leadership. Political victories that undermine trust in politics shouldn't be considered victories; they're net losses for society. Record corporate profits achieved by eroding the public's trust in business aren't successes;

they're derelictions of duty. Lobbying and campaign donations that result in laws and regulations favoring the lobbyists and donors aren't triumphs if they weaken public confidence in our democracy; they, too, are abject failures of leadership.

But how can leaders buck the pressures to do whatever it takes to win when *not* doing so allows their political or economic competitors to prevail, and puts them out of a job? This has become the standard justification for whatever-it-takes leadership. Yet it's based on a fallacy. It assumes that the backers who put such people into positions of leadership—voters, investors, members of various organizations—intend for them to do whatever it takes to win.

Many of these backers, however, do not want leaders to do whatever it takes, because they understand their *own* obligations to the common good, and how such strategies harm everyone over the longer term. True leaders must help more people to understand this. One example: On the eve of the Senate's final vote on repealing the Affordable Care Act in July 2017, Senator John McCain returned to Washington from his home in Arizona, where he was being treated for brain cancer, to cast the deciding vote against repeal. But that was not the most important thing he did. He took to the Senate floor to condemn the whatever-it-takes politics that had overtaken Washington. McCain began by saluting a former generation of senators for whom the common good was more important than winning any particular legislative contest. "I've known and admired men and women in the Senate who played much more than a small role in our history, true states- men, giants of American politics," he said.

> They came from both parties, and from various backgrounds. Their ambitions were frequently in conflict. They held different views on the issues of the day. And they often had very serious disagree- ments about how best to serve the national inter- est. But they knew that however sharp and heartfelt their disputes, however keen their ambitions, they had an obligation to work collaboratively to ensure the Senate discharged its constitutional responsibili- ties effectively. . . . That principled mindset, and the service of our predecessors who possessed it, come to mind when I hear the Senate referred to as the world's greatest deliberative body.

McCain then admonished his present colleagues for eroding the common good, with words aimed as much at voters as at the senators. "Our deliberations today . . . are more partisan, more tribal, more of the time than any other time I remember," he said. He reminded them that winning was not as important as upholding and strength- ening the institutions of governing.

> Our system doesn't depend on our nobility. It accounts for our imperfections, and gives an order to our individual strivings that has helped make

ours the most powerful and prosperous society on earth. It is our responsibility to preserve that, even when it requires us to do something less satisfying than "winning." Even when we must give a little to get a little. Even when our efforts manage just three yards and a cloud of dust, while critics on both sides denounce us for timidity, for our failure to "triumph."

This wasn't the first time McCain refused to pander to the worst in current American politics, even though pandering might have been an easier path to victory. One of my fondest memories of McCain occurred in the 2008 presidential campaign, at a town hall event in Minnesota when he responded to a supporter who said he was "scared" at the prospect of an Obama presidency. "I have to tell you," McCain said, "Senator Obama is a decent person and a person you don't have to be scared of as president of the United States." At this, the Republican crowd booed. "Come on, John!" one audience member yelled out. Others shouted that Obama was a "liar" and a "terrorist." A woman holding a microphone said, "I can't trust Obama. I have read about him and he's not, he's not uh—he's an Arab. He's not . . ." At that moment McCain snapped the microphone from her hand and replied, "No, ma'am. He's a decent family man [and] citizen that I just happen to have disagreements with on fundamental issues and that's what this campaign's all about. He's not [an Arab]."

Our best chance of reversing whatever-it-takes politics is through political leaders like John McCain who demand that politicians attend to the common good rather than win by undermining it—and who help educate the public about the importance of doing exactly this. This is the essence of political leadership.

In 2017, Arizona senator Jeff Flake demonstrated similar leadership (what is it about Arizona?) when he castigated his fellow Republicans for their failure to stand up to Trump. To carry on "as if what was happening was anything approaching normalcy required a determined suspension of critical faculties. And tremendous powers of denial," Flake wrote. "If by 2017 the conservative bargain was to go along for the very bumpy ride because with congressional hegemony and the White House we had the numbers to achieve some long-held policy goals—even as we put at risk our institutions and our values—then it was a very real question whether any such policy victories wouldn't be Pyrrhic ones." Flake reminded Americans that politics must be about strengthening the institutions of self-government. He went on: "If this was our Faustian bargain, then it was not worth it. If ultimately our principles were so malleable as to no longer be principles, then what was the point of political victories in the first place?" Flake warned that conservatives had taken the institutions of government for granted "as we have engaged in one of the more reckless periods of politics in our history. In 2017, we seem to have lost our appreciation for just how hard won and vulnerable those institutions are."

I don't want to suggest it has only been Republicans who have admonished their leaders over whatever-it-takes politics. In October 2015, during the Democrats' primary debate, Virginia senator Jim Webb was asked how, if he were elected president, he would govern differently from Barack Obama. Webb said the difference would be "the use of executive authority." Webb said he objected to Obama's tendency to make laws through executive orders. The practice hurt our system of government. "I came up as a committee counsel in the Congress, used to put dozens of bills through the House floor every year as a committee counsel," Webb said. "I have very strong feelings about how our federal system works and how we need to lead and energize the congressional process instead of allowing these divisions to continue to paralyze what we're doing. So I would lead—working with both parties in the Congress and working through them in the traditional way that our Constitution is set."

Whatever-it-takes politics comes at a huge cost to the common good. That cost is often hidden. McCain, Flake, and Webb brought some of it into the light.

An American president is not just the chief executive of the United States, and the office he (eventually she) holds is not just a bully pulpit to advance certain policy ideas. He is also a moral leader, and the office is a moral pulpit invested with meaning about the common good. It is hardly the case that every president has been a moral exemplar, but a president inevitably helps set the moral tone of the nation. The values a president enunciates and demonstrates ricochet through society, strengthening or undermining the common good.

As one of George Washington's biographers, Douglas Southall Freeman, explained, Washington believed he had been entrusted with something of immense intrinsic worth, and that his duty was to uphold it for its own sake and over the long term. Even by June 1775, when Congress appointed him to command the nation's army, Washington had already "become a moral rallying post, the embodiment of the purpose, the patience, and the determination necessary for the triumph of the revolutionary cause. He had retained the support of Congress and won that of New England in like manner and measure, by directness, by deference, and by manifest dedication to duty." Washington exemplified a duty to the cause of the Constitution and liberty. He led by moral example.

Some 240 years later, in the 2016 presidential campaign, candidate Donald Trump was accused of failing to pay his income taxes. His response was, "That makes me smart." Although not yet president, his comment conveyed a message to millions of other Americans that paying taxes in full is not an obligation of citizenship. As I've pointed out, Trump also boasted about giving money to politicians so they would do whatever he wanted. "When they call, I give. And you know what, when I need something from them two years later, three years later, I call them. They are there for me." In other words, it's perfectly okay for business leaders to pay off politicians, regardless of the effect on our democracy.

Trump sent another message by refusing to reveal his tax returns during the campaign or even when he took office, or to put his businesses into a blind trust to avoid conflicts of interest, and by his overt willingness to make money off his presidency by having foreign diplomats stay at his Washington hotel, and promoting his various golf clubs. These were not just ethical lapses. They directly undermined the common good by reducing the public's trust in the office of the president. As *The New York Times* editorial board put it in June 2017, "For Mr. Trump and his circle, what matters is not what's right but what you can get away with. In his White House, if you're avoiding the appearance of impropriety, you're not pushing the boundaries hard enough. Government ethics officials say dealing with this administration is an exhausting game of whack-a-mole: go after one potential violation, and two others crop up. That's because ethical regulations were not written with this sort of administration in mind."

A president's most fundamental responsibility is to uphold and protect our system of government. Trump has weakened that system. When, as a presidential nominee, he said that a particular federal judge shouldn't be hearing a case against him because the judge's parents were Mexican, Trump did more than insult a member of the judiciary; he attacked the impartiality of America's legal system. When Trump threatened to "loosen" federal libel laws so he could sue news organizations that were critical of him and, later, to revoke the licenses of networks critical of him, he wasn't just bullying the media; he was threatening the freedom and integrity of the press. When, as president, he equated neo-Nazis and Ku Klux Klan members with counter-demonstrators in Charlottesville, Virginia, by blaming "both sides" for the violence, he wasn't being neutral. He was condoning white supremacists, thereby undermining equal rights. When he pardoned Joe Arpaio, the former sheriff of Maricopa County, Arizona, for a criminal contempt conviction, he wasn't just signaling it's okay for the police to engage in brutal violations of civil rights; he was also subverting the rule of law by impairing the judiciary's power to force public officials to abide by court decisions. When he criticized NFL players for kneeling during the national anthem, he wasn't just asking that they demonstrate their patriotism; he was disrespecting their—and, indirectly, everyone's—freedom of speech. In all these ways, Trump undermined core values of our democracy.

Steve Kerr, coach of the NBA's Golden State Warriors, responded to Trump's attack on the NFL players by using Kerr's own position of authority to reframe what the players were doing. "Just think about what those players are protesting," said Kerr.

They're protesting excessive police violence and racial inequality. Those are really good things to fight against. And they're doing it in a nonviolent way. Which is everything that Martin Luther King preached, right? A lot of American military members will tell you that the right to free speech is exactly what they fight for. And it's just really, really upsetting that the leader of our country is calling for these players to be "fired."

Kerr went on to urge Trump to use his moral authority as president to unite rather than divide.

The fact is we live in an amazing country, but it's a flawed one. I consider myself unbelievably lucky to live here, so please spare me the "If you don't like it you can get out" argument. I love living here. I love my country. I just think it's important to recognize that we as a nation are far from perfect, and it's our responsibility to try to make it better. And one of the ways to do that is to promote awareness and understanding and acceptance. Not just acceptance but embracing our diversity, which when you get down to it is not only who we are but truly what makes us great. And it's not happening. Remember, the president works for us, not vice versa. We elected him. He doesn't just work for his constituents and his base. He works for every citizen. Once you take that office, you have to do what's best for the entire country. Sure, you're going to have policies that align with your party, but that's not the point. Respectfully, Mr. Trump, the point is this: You're the president. You represent all of us. Don't divide us. Bring us together.

. . .

The mere fact that someone has become president of the United States itself lends his views public legitimacy. A team of economists led by Leonardo Bursztyn of the University of Chicago showed that Trump's harangues against immigrants during the 2016 presidential election helped legitimize anti-immigrant bigotry. Two weeks before the election, Bursztyn and his colleagues recruited 458 people from eight states where Trump was leading. Half were told Trump would definitely win; the other half got no information about Trump's projected victory. The researchers then asked each of them whether they would authorize the researchers to donate $1 to a group called the Federation for American Immigration Reform, which the researchers described (accurately) as an anti-immigrant organization whose founder wants European Americans to remain the majority in the United States. Half were assured their decision would be anonymous; the other half assumed it could become public. For those who were not informed about Trump's expected victory in their state, donating to the anti-immigration group was far more attractive when their anonymity was assured than when they thought they might be exposed (54 percent authorized the donation if secret, 34 percent if it might go public). But among participants who were told Trump would win, half authorized the donation regardless of anonymity.

While many Americans harbored anti-immigrant feelings before Trump, they kept those feelings to themselves.

Perhaps they didn't even allow them to rise to full consciousness. That's because such sentiments were assumed to be wrong—to violate the common good. But Trump's election legitimized those sentiments because it suggested that millions of others shared them. After Trump, bigotry became more acceptable.

So did bashing political opponents even after an election is over. Before Trump, the peaceful transfer of power was assumed to be a central feature of our democracy. As Harvard political scientist Archon Fung has noted, when losing candidates congratulate winners and deliver gracious concession speeches, they demonstrate their commitment to the democratic system over any specific outcomes they fought to achieve. That demonstration is an important means of reestablishing civility. Think of Al Gore's gracious concession speech to George W. Bush in 2000, after five weeks of a bitterly contested election and just one day after the Supreme Court ruled 5–4 in favor of Bush: "I say to President-elect Bush that what remains of partisan rancor must now be put aside, and may God bless his stewardship of this country. . . . Neither he nor I anticipated this long and difficult road. Certainly neither of us wanted it to happen. Yet it came, and now it has ended resolved, as it must be resolved, through the honored institutions of our democracy. . . . Now the U.S. Supreme Court has spoken. Let there be no doubt, while I strongly disagree with the court's decision, I accept it. . . . And tonight, for the sake of our unity as a people and the strength of our democracy, I offer my concession."

Bush's response was no less gracious: "Vice President Gore and I put our hearts and hopes into our campaigns; we both gave it our all. We shared similar emotions. I understand how difficult this moment must be for Vice President Gore and his family. He has a distinguished record of service to our country as a congressman, a senator, and as vice president. This evening I received a gracious call from the vice president. We agreed to meet early next week in Washington and we agreed to do our best to heal our country after this hard-fought contest. . . . Americans share hopes and goals and values far more important than any political disagreements. Republicans want the best for our nation. And so do Democrats. Our votes may differ, but not our hopes."

Many voters continued to doubt the legitimacy of Bush's victory, but there was no civil war. Think of what might have occurred if Gore had bitterly accused Bush of winning fraudulently, and blamed the five Republican appointees on the Supreme Court for siding with Bush for partisan reasons. Think what might have happened if, during his campaign, Bush had promised to put Gore in jail for various improprieties, and then, after he won, accused Gore (or Bill Clinton) of spying on him during the campaign and trying to use the FBI and CIA to bring about his downfall. These statements—close to ones that Donald Trump actually made—might have imperiled the political stability of the nation. They would have sacrificed the common good to an extreme form of whatever-it-takes politics. Instead, Gore and Bush made the same moral choice their predecessors had made at the end of every previous American presidential election, and for the same reason: They understood that the peaceful transition of power confirmed the nation's commitment to the Constitution, which was far more important than their own losses or wins. It was a matter of public morality. Trump had no such concern.

This is the essence of Trump's failure of trusteeship—not that he has chosen one set of policies over another, or has divided rather than united Americans, or even that he has behaved in childish and vindictive ways unbecoming a president. It is that he has sacrificed the processes and institutions of American democracy to achieve his goals. By saying and doing whatever it takes to win, he has abused the trust we place in a president to preserve and protect the nation's capacity for self-government.

CEOs and directors of major corporations are also entrusted with the common good. It is no excuse for them to argue they have no choice but to do whatever it takes to maximize share prices. No law requires them to do this. As I've shown, the idea that the sole purpose of a corporation is to maximize share prices is relatively new, dating back to the 1980s. The dominant view for decades before had been that corporations are responsible to all their stakeholders.

In the summer of 2014, the managers, employees, and customers of a New England chain of supermarkets called Market Basket joined together to oppose the board of

directors' decision earlier that year to oust the chain's popular chief executive, Arthur T. Demoulas. Their demonstrations and boycotts emptied most of the chain's seventy
stores. What had been special about Arthur T, as he was
known, was his approach to business. He kept prices lower
than his competitors, paid his employees more, and gave
them and his managers more authority to make decisions.
Just before he was ousted he offered customers an additional 4 percent discount, arguing they could make better
use of the money than the shareholders could. Arthur T
viewed Market Basket as a joint enterprise from which
everyone should benefit, not just its shareholders—which
was why the board fired him. Yet eventually consumers
and employees won. The boycott was so costly that the
board sold the company to Arthur T.

CEOs of big corporations might say Market Basket
doesn't apply to them because it's not a publicly held company whose shares are traded on major stock exchanges.
Market Basket doesn't have to worry about failing to maximize share prices, and thereby succumb to corporate raiders or activist investors. True, but this doesn't let CEOs of
publicly traded companies off the hook. Arthur T's business model could be applied even where many shareholders are involved. Patagonia, a large apparel manufacturer
based in Ventura, California, for example, has organized
itself as a "benefit corporation"—a for-profit company
whose articles of incorporation require that it take into
account the interests of workers, the community, and the
environment, as well as shareholders. Benefit corporations

are certified and their performance is regularly reviewed by nonprofit third-party entities, such as B Lab. By 2017, thirty-one states had enacted laws allowing companies to incorporate in this way, thereby giving CEOs and directors explicit legal authority to consider the interest of all stakeholders.

CEOs might still argue that if they want to raise money in public capital markets they have to attend solely to the interests of shareholders, or else competitive forces will wipe them out. That argument makes it sound as if CEOs are powerless to change this. But recall that markets are based on rules, and human beings create those rules. Remember also that CEOs of large companies have outsized political influence over what those rules are. CEOs who understand leadership as trusteeship could use their outsized political influence to push for laws that resurrect stakeholder capitalism—requiring CEOs to consider all their stakeholders; giving workers greater voice in management decisions, as in Germany; requiring companies to make "severance payments" to communities they abandon, in order to compensate for the disruption; prohibiting mandatory arbitration in contracts with customers and employees; and limiting the tax deductibility of CEO pay.

Why stop there? Why don't CEOs of big companies do whatever they can to make the economy work for everyone rather than for a privileged few like themselves? Rather than reflexively seek tax cuts, they could push to raise taxes on corporations as well as on people like themselves and other wealthy Americans, and dedicate the funds to better schools for all American kids. They could seek a higher minimum wage, bigger wage subsidies (in the form of the Earned Income Tax Credit), better infrastructure, more portable pensions, universal health care, and other measures that would raise wages and make American workers more economically secure. Rather than fight for laws that make it harder for workers to unionize, they could fight for laws that make it easier.

If this sounds far-fetched, that's only because of how far we've come from the era when the heads of American business viewed themselves as "corporate statesmen" with responsibilities for the common good. In the 1940s and 1950s, CEOs of major corporations like General Motors, Coca-Cola, and Eastman Kodak joined together in the Committee for Economic Development, to lobby for measures to expand jobs. They even argued that unions "serve the common good." In the 1960s, many of these CEOs lobbied for stronger environmental protections, and for passage of the Environmental Protection Act.

As I've noted, most Americans now believe the system is rigged in favor of big corporations and Wall Street, and in many respects it is. But nothing is stopping CEOs and top executives on Wall Street from putting an end to the rigging. They could reduce the needs of candidates to raise vast sums of campaign money by supporting public financing of campaigns. They could back stricter limits on the "revolving door" between industry and government personnel, and laws requiring full disclosure of the sources of all campaign funding. Why shouldn't CEOs and top Wall Street executives be in the vanguard of seeking a constitutional amendment allowing lawmakers to limit lobbying and campaign spending?

The answer is: Nothing is stopping them, except their own parched, self-serving notion of leadership as maximizing profits and shareholder value, whatever it takes. But as leaders of institutions with the greatest influence over American politics, they also have a duty to the common good and are uniquely positioned to advance it. For too long they have abdicated this responsibility. We are now living with the consequences. They can see these consequences as readily as you can, if they're willing to look.

None of this is simply a matter of "ethics." Ethics involves fulfilling legal responsibilities, avoiding obvious conflicts of interest, and behaving in an aboveboard manner. As now routinely taught in graduate schools of business and as required for obtaining many professional licenses, ethics is about how to avoid legal troubles or public relations disasters. Leadership as trusteeship extends way beyond ethics. It goes to the heart of the job. It requires a different way of thinking about the central obligation of leading any institution. Part of the responsibility of elected or appointed government officials, of corporate executives, and of leaders of nonprofits and other major organizations in society must be to enhance the public's trust in their institutions and in our political economic system as a whole. Their success should not be measured solely in how much money they or their organizations make or raise, how much power they accumulate, or how much influence they wield. They must also be judged by the legacy of trust they pass onward. As Shimon Peres, a former prime minister and president of Israel, put it in his memoir, "We need a generation that sees leadership as a noble cause, defined not by personal ambition, but by morality and a call to service." Exactly. The purpose of leadership is not simply to win. It is to serve.

CHAPTER 8

Honor and Shame

SOCIETIES TRADITIONALLY ENFORCE the common good through honor and shame—honoring those who make exemplary contributions to it and shaming those who exploit it for personal gain. Can we do so again? Ideally, children learn about honor and shame at an early age by watching and hearing parents, teachers, mentors, and religious leaders. Adults help a young child develop a moral consciousness through how they live their lives, whom they admire and respect, and whose behavior they disdain. Some of these lessons are also conveyed by one generation to the next in morality tales—the Bible or other sacred texts, histories and prominent biographies, and fictionalized stories of heroism and treachery. Other lessons are embedded in popular culture—songs, movies, biographies, and the daily news. As I've said, a president of the United States has a special role because he or she is a living embodiment of honor or shame. These lessons establish and reconfirm the common good, not as propaganda but as the expression of a society's values.

Tribal cultures live by honor and shame. These sentiments also play a large role in certain Asian societies. Since the founding of the United States, as I have noted, religious communities have informed people's understandings of what they owe to one another as participants in the same community. These influences can be powerful because one of humankind's deepest needs is to *belong*. Through most of human history survival has depended on extended families, clans, and tribes. To be highly respected has meant strong support from the group. Historically, to be ostracized has often meant death.

Modern America seems to have misplaced honor and shame. We often honor people who haven't advanced the common good but have merely achieved notoriety or celebrity, or amassed great wealth or power. We shame people not for having exploited the common good for personal gain but for failing to conform to prevailing ideas about fashion or coolness, or for associating with the wrong people.

If we're to revive the common good we must use honor and shame appropriately, bringing public attention to virtuous behavior and public condemnation to behavior that erodes public trust. Doing this, of course, can be tricky. If shame is to be meaningful, average people must retain their capacity to be offended by actions that undermine the common good. If they tip over into cynicism or become numbed to such behavior, they may no longer see it as particularly shameful. The behavior becomes normalized. It's also the case that people who have shown utter contempt for the common good are often the least capable of feeling shame. They are literally shameless. During his trial for criminal fraud, Martin Shkreli ridiculed prosecutors; after his conviction, he smirked.

By the same token, some of the most truly honorable people in society don't seek honors. Their modesty and humility often make them nearly invisible. They credit others, and respect their craft or calling too much to think of themselves as exemplary or extraordinary. Hugh Heclo relates a speech given by Chicago Cub Ryne Sandberg when he was inducted into the Baseball Hall of Fame in 2005: "I was in awe every time I walked onto the field," Sandberg said.

> That's respect. I was taught you never, ever disrespect your opponents or your teammates or your organization or your manager and never, ever your uniform. Make a great play, act like you've done it before; get a big hit, look for the third base coach and get ready to run the bases; hit a home run, put your head down, drop the bat, run around the bases, because the name on the front is a lot more important than the name on the back.

Sandberg credited others who had been inducted before him:

> These guys sitting up here did not pave the way for the rest of us so that players could swing for

the fences every time up and forget how to move a runner over to third. It's disrespectful to them, to you, and to the game of baseball that we all played growing up. Respect. A lot of people say this honor validates my career, but I didn't work hard for validation. I didn't play the game right because I saw a reward at the end of the tunnel. I played it right because that's what you're supposed to do, play it right and with respect.... If this validates anything, it's that guys who taught me the game ... did what they were supposed to do, and I did what I was supposed to do.

Honor and shame can be dangerous sentiments in the wrong hands or if used for the wrong purposes. Dictators and demagogues throughout history have bestowed honors on those loyal to them and sought to disgrace those with the courage to stand up to them. Public shaming can also carry a painful stigma. "Ignominy is universally acknowledged to be a worse punishment than death," wrote Benjamin Rush, a signer of the Declaration of Independence who also sought to put an end to public stocks and whipping posts. Four centuries ago, public shaming included scarlet A's. In the 1950s, Senator Joseph McCarthy destroyed reputations and careers by accusing people of being communists. These days, social media can unleash torrents of invective upon people who do little more than say something silly or insensitive, or who look different. It can cause a sensitive teenager to take his or her life.

. . .

In contemporary America, the meaning of honor has become confused partly because those who bestow honors often have ulterior motives. Government funding has dried up for nonprofits such as universities, hospitals, and museums. Funds for social services of churches and community groups are growing scarce. Appropriations for public television, the arts, museums, and libraries have been slashed. Research grants are waning. Legislatures are cutting back on university funding. Meanwhile, vast riches have been accumulating in the hands of a relative few. As a result of both trends, nonprofits have been using the lure of honors to hook rich donors. Presidents of universities, congregations, think tanks, and other nonprofits are now kissing the posteriors of wealthy donors as never before. Galas are held in their honor. Colleges bestow on them honorary degrees. Endowed professorships carry their names. They are awarded prizes and medals. Awards and prizes themselves are named in their honor. University buildings, concert halls, and museums are also named after them, their family names etched for eternity in granite or marble. In all these ways their identities become synonymous with society's notions of honorability.

Curiously, though, little or no attention is given to how these donors obtained their wealth. They may have violated or skirted laws, paid off politicians, engaged in insider trading or price-fixing, defrauded investors, or even brought the world economy to near ruin because of their disregard for the consequences of their schemes. These behaviors, though, are assumed to be irrelevant to the deal at hand: In return for their donation, they are imbued with moral approval. The subtle message is that the common good doesn't really count. Wealth and power do.

The aforementioned Michael Milken was indicted in 1989 for racketeering and securities fraud. He pleaded guilty to securities and reporting violations and was sentenced to ten years in prison (subsequently reduced to two), a fine of $600 million, and a permanent ban from the securities industry. In 2016, the very same man was honored with the Dr. Armand Hammer Philanthropy Award. "I don't think . . . prostate cancer research would be where it is today without Michael Milken," gushed former film studio executive Sherry Lansing at the award ceremony. "He is the pioneer in this field, so I'm incredibly grateful to him in all areas of cancer research. He's extraordinarily generous."

Milken's generosity was admirable, but bestowing a public honor on him required that the benefactors suspend any moral judgment about how his wealth had been obtained. It is an example of the intentional unawareness that conservative writer and former education secretary William Bennett had once warned about. "Nonjudgementalism . . . has permeated our culture," he wrote, "encouraging a paralysis of the moral faculty." It would be one thing if Milken had publicly admitted that his fraudulent acts were wrong and then openly sought to redeem himself through philanthropy. At least then the subsequent honors wouldn't seem so at odds with the common good. But to the contrary, he heaped praise on himself for what he did. In 2017, his webpage claimed that his "use of convertible bonds, preferred stock, high-yield bonds, collateralized loans, equity-linked instruments, securitized obligations and derivatives, among other instruments, helped create millions of jobs, leading a *Time* bureau chief to write, in 1997, 'Milken was right in almost every sense.'"

Sometimes these deals put their beneficiaries in the awkward position of having to defend the honor of philanthropists tainted by scandal. The Taubman Center at Harvard's Kennedy School of Government is named after Alfred Taubman, who in 1988 donated $15 million to establish it. In 2002, Taubman was sentenced to prison for orchestrating a price-fixing scheme between the nation's top two auction houses. After the conviction, Harvard students asked Harvard officials whether they would change the name of the center. The answer was no. The center's director explained that "in the great scheme of things, [Taubman] has led a very ethical life. His conviction does not mean that his life has not been ethical, or one that Harvard doesn't want to associate with." Hello? Taubman had just been convicted of price-fixing. His name was etched on Harvard's school of *government*, which is supposed to train students to work for the common good. A criminal conviction for price-fixing did not alter the appropriateness of honoring this man?

At other times, such deals confer on donors a patina of respectability and social approval that obscures the donors' ongoing attacks on the common good. Consider David Koch, co-owner, with his brother, Charles, of Koch Industries. In 2008, the New York City Ballet renamed its home at Lincoln Center the David H. Koch Theater after he donated $100 million to modernize it. "The renaming acknowledges the extraordinary generosity of Mr. Koch," said a spokesperson for the ballet. To my knowledge, David Koch has broken no law, but his political activities have undoubtedly undermined the common good. I'm not talking about the Koch brothers' right-wing political views. People may differ in their opinions about taxes or the environment. It's that the Koch brothers' political spending has been so vast that it has made a mockery of the ideal of equal voting rights. As Charles Lewis, founder of the Center for Public Integrity, a nonpartisan watchdog group, told *The New Yorker*'s Jane Mayer, "The Kochs are on a whole different level. There's no one else who has spent this much money. The sheer dimension of it is what sets them apart. They have a pattern of law-breaking, political manipulation, and obfuscation. I've been in Washington since Watergate, and I've never seen anything like it. They are the Standard Oil of our times." Early in 2017, a spokesman for the Kochs' political network said it planned to spend between $300 million and $400 million to influence politics and public policy during the first two years of the Trump administration.

Public honors are similarly lavished on celebrities—people sufficiently well known that the act of honoring them generates positive publicity for the institution and

assures current and prospective donors of its importance. In return, the celebrity gets an honorary degree or
an embossed plaque or, sometimes, even money (appropriately called an "honorarium") for attending. In many
instances, the celebrity is repaying a friend or business
associate (say, a movie producer who happens to serve
on the board of the conferring institution). The transac-
tion is innocent enough. No overt harm is done. But in
the process, the idea of "honor" is debased. The celebrity is
already celebrated, by definition. He or she is being honored for being celebrated, a tautology that displaces any
intervening thought about the common good.

Honors should matter, especially when they appear
to convey social judgment. We automatically attach the
prefix "the honorable" to the names of presidents, vice
presidents, members of both houses of Congress, judges,
and other people appointed to office nominated by the
president and confirmed by the Senate (except for military
officers). Once the title is conferred, the recipient keeps
it for the remainder of her life. By some estimates, nearly
100,000 people in the United States are addressed as "the
honorable." I don't mean to sound priggish, but I don't
see why members of Congress who have been convicted
of taking bribes or embezzling money should continue
to be referred to as "the honorable"—nor, for that matter,
any members who have been censured or reprimanded by
their colleagues. Why should a cabinet member convicted
of breaking the law while in office remain "the honorable," even if he subsequently receives a presidential par-

don? Why should a member of Congress who beats up a reporter for asking a question he doesn't like be referred to as "the honorable"? Their behavior was shameful. They've dishonored themselves and the offices they held in trust.

Those who are honored should have shown the courage to stand up for the common good against the forces of greed, corruption, and abuse of power. I'm thinking of people like Cheryl Eckard, who, in 2002, as a quality assurance manager at pharmaceutical giant GlaxoSmithKline, discovered serious problems at its largest plant—drugs produced in nonsterile environments, a water system contaminated with microorganisms, and medicines made in the wrong doses. After Eckard alerted management, she was fired. She then shared her findings with the Food and Drug Administration, and sued the company. After an eight-year trial, GlaxoSmithKline agreed to pay the government $750 million for manufacturing and selling adulterated drug products. The court also ordered the firm to compensate Eckard for her dismissal and the emotional harm it caused her. "It's difficult to survive this financially, emotionally, you lose all your friends, because all your friends are people you have at work," Eckard said afterward. "You really do have to understand that it's a very difficult process but very well worth it."

We should also honor people like Army Major General Antonio Taguba, who insisted on an honest investigation into the alleged torture of prisoners by the CIA and U.S.

Army at the Abu Ghraib prison in Iraq even though his military and political superiors didn't want one. "From the moment a soldier enlists, we inculcate loyalty, duty, honor, integrity, and selfless service," said Taguba. "And yet when we get to the senior-officer level we forget these values. . . . The fact is that we violated the laws of land warfare in Abu Ghraib. We violated the tenets of the Geneva Convention. We violated our own principles, and we violated the core of our military values."

We should honor Eileen Foster, who in 2008, while in charge of fraud investigations at Countrywide Financial Corporation (the nation's largest subprime mortgage lender at the epicenter of the mortgage meltdown that almost brought the entire economy to its knees), told her superiors that many executives in Countrywide's chain of command were working to cover up the massive fraud. A few months later, Countrywide's new owner, Bank of America, fired her for "unprofessional conduct." Foster then began a three-year fight to clear her name and prove she and other employees had been punished for doing the right thing. In 2010, the U.S. Department of Labor ruled that Bank of America had illegally fired her for exposing the fraud. "I don't let people bully me, intimidate me, and coerce me," Foster told the Center for Public Integrity's *iWatch News*. "And it's just not right that people don't know what happened here and how it happened."

I'm also thinking about people who have quietly and modestly worked for the common good over long periods of time, in ways that have made all of us better off or more secure—public servants like Daniel Fried, to whom I referred earlier, who joined the Foreign Service in 1977 and served for forty years. Fried rarely made the headlines. Instead, he quietly demonstrated the importance of steady diplomacy and patient engagement with the rest of the world.

We should honor unsung heroes like John Mindermann and Paul Magallanes, the FBI agents who were on duty when they received word of a break-in at the Democratic National Committee headquarters at the Watergate complex in 1972. Years later, Mindermann remembered Nixon's aides who tried to stonewall their investigation as "gutless and completely self-serving. They lacked the ability to do the right thing." Mindermann and Magallanes had no doubt that the right thing was to bring that wrongdoing to light. As Magallanes recounted to *The New York Times*, "It was we, the FBI, who brought Richard Nixon down. We showed that our government can investigate itself."

Let me add to the honor roll people who put themselves in harm's way for the good of all—first responders, volunteers in natural disasters, firefighters, police officers, members of the armed forces. We should also honor others who do just about the most difficult jobs of all, often in harrowing circumstances—teachers in poor communities, social workers, nurses, elder-care and hospice workers. They are the true heroes of America. They keep the nation going. But they're often overlooked, sometimes even insulted. Most earn very little. Isn't it time we honored them?

We can honor them with our respect and appreciation. We can honor them by making sure they earn enough money to live on. We can also honor them by raising public awareness of the importance of the work they do. We have Academy Awards for actors, directors, and screenwriters; Nobel Prizes in math and science; culinary awards for chefs; Olympic awards for athletes; Kennedy Center honors for the performing arts. Why not awards for upholding and strengthening the common good? A Common Good Award for an outstanding whistle-blower. A Common Good Award for an exemplary civil servant. A Common Good Award for the teacher or social worker whose quiet and modest work over the course of her career has dramatically improved other people's lives. A Common Good Award for the nonprofit leader who has taken a courageous stand speaking truth to power.

Why shouldn't universities confer honorary degrees on these unsung American heroes? Why doesn't the United States, as does Britain, issue honors to a thousand citizens each year who have made significant contributions to the common good? Their purpose would be to continually remind us of what it means to work for the common good, to offer examples of civic behavior we want to encourage, and to raise public consciousness of what we owe each other as members of the same society. Such public honoring could be a corrective to what we now do—blindly and automatically bestow honors on rich philanthropists because they're rich, and celebrities because they're celebrated.

·   ·   ·

Wielded appropriately, shame can also be a powerful motivator for the common good. It can illuminate the gap between the ideals we profess and the reality we tolerate, mobilizing us into action. Martin Luther King, Jr., shamed the nation by making it impossible for white Americans outside the South to condemn segregation there while at the same time tolerating discrimination all around them. As King told a crowd of 25,000 in Detroit in June 1963, two months before his historic speech in Washington,

> We've got to come to see that the problem of racial injustice is a national problem. No community in this country can boast of clean hands in the area of brotherhood. Now in the North it's different in that it doesn't have the legal sanction that it has in the South. But it has its subtle and hidden forms and it exists in three areas: in the area of employment discrimination, in the area of housing discrimination and *de facto* segregation in the public schools. And we must come to see that *de facto* segregation in the North is just as injurious as the actual segregation in the South. And so if you want to help us in Alabama and Mississippi and all over the South, do all that you can to get rid of the problem here.

By extending the shame of Southern segregation to the nation as a whole, King raised the bar: We were all implicated in racial discrimination. Racial segregation was the North's shame as well as the South's. It continues to be.

Another version of this sort of shaming occurred in 1954 when Joseph Welch, then chief council for the U.S. Army, stood up to Senator Joseph McCarthy before a nationwide television audience. During a hearing in which McCarthy accused the army of harboring communists, McCarthy attacked one of Welch's young assistants, Fred Fisher, for having once belonged to the National Lawyers Guild, which McCarthy considered a communist front. Welch responded: "Until this moment, Senator, I think I have never really gauged your cruelty or your recklessness." As McCarthy renewed his attack on Fisher, Welch interrupted him. "Senator, may we not drop this? We know he belonged to the Lawyers Guild. . . . Let us not assassinate this lad further, Senator. You've done enough. Have you no sense of decency, sir? At long last, have you left no sense of decency?" McCarthy tried to make another point about Fisher, but Welch stopped him again. "I will not discuss this further with you. You have sat within six feet of me and could have asked me about Fred Fisher. You have seen fit to bring it out. And if there is a God in Heaven it will do neither you nor your cause any good. I will not discuss it further. . . . You, Mr. Chairman, may, if you will, call the next witness."

At this point the audience inside the hearing room broke into applause, and millions of Americans watching the proceedings from their living rooms saw McCarthy as the dangerous bully he was. By shaming McCarthy, Welch shamed America for having tolerated McCarthy and the communist witch hunt he was leading. That was the beginning of the end of McCarthy's reign of terror, and of America's paranoia about communist enemies within.

A more recent example occurred in August 2017 after Donald Trump equated the neo-Nazis who marched on Charlottesville, Virginia, with counter-demonstrators there. In response to Trump's equivocation, Kenneth Frazier, the head of Merck pharmaceuticals, resigned from Trump's business advisory council, the first CEO to do so. Frazier said that "America's leaders must honor our fundamental values by clearly rejecting expressions of hatred, bigotry, and group supremacy, which run counter to the American ideal that all people are created equal. As CEO of Merck and as a matter of personal conscience, I feel a responsibility to take a stand against intolerance and extremism." Frazier's words and action fortified other CEOs to follow him in resigning from Trump's advisory boards. Although Trump himself has shown no capacity for shame, their action had large symbolic importance. It signified that the corporate leaders of America were not going to abide white supremacists. They were going to take a stand for the ideal of racial equality.

Shame may be in our genes, helping us survive. Charles Darwin, in his book *The Expression of the Emotions in Man and Animals,* noted that humans around the world express shame in similar ways—blushing, becoming hot, casting their eyes downward, and lowering their heads. Shame may have evolved as a way to maintain social trust necessary for the survival of a group and, therefore, of its members. In a 2012 paper, psychologists Matthew Feinberg and Dacher Keltner and sociologist Robb Willer found evidence that embarrassment—which often accompanies shame—functions socially as a kind of "nonverbal apology" for having done something that violates group norms. A display of embarrassment shows others that the embarrassed person is still aware of the group's expectations and is still committed to the group's well-being.

But in modern America we often shame the wrong people. Instead of deterring behavior that undermines the common good, shame is too often deployed against people who don't fit in—to ostracize them even further. That has happened on social media through "cyberbullying."

Even when it comes to truly shameful acts, the ability of anyone to use social media to accuse anyone else of committing them can have unfair and destructive consequences. After white supremacists marched on Charlottesville, onlookers shared hundreds of photos of them online. This form of shaming may have deterred some white supremacists from participating in future marches. But in this case, some people who hadn't been involved in the march were accused of marching because of their likeness to someone who had been. An assistant professor at the University of Arkansas School of Engineering who resembled a white supremacist at the rally was misidentified as a participant, and received a torrent of threatening messages. If the common good is to be revived, shame must be used carefully and accurately.

Even when the right people are shamed, there must be appropriate consequences. Members of Congress often make demonstrations of shaming CEOs who have harmed the common good, but they're typically no more than shaming rituals for the cameras. Hearings have been staged to berate CEOs of tobacco companies, oil companies, auto companies, Big Pharma, and Wall Street—even Martin Shkreli and Wells Fargo's John Stumpf—but the scolding merely creates an illusion of accountability. After Shkreli's appearance, Congress didn't take action to prevent drug-price gouging. After Stumpf appeared, Congress didn't pass legislation making it harder for banks to defraud their customers, and Stumpf was never prosecuted.

When the carelessness of oil company BP on the North Slope led to the temporary shutdown of the nation's largest oilfield, in August 2006, Congress demanded BP executives appear in person to answer for it. Representative Joe Barton, a Texas Republican and vice chairman of the Committee on Energy and Commerce, excoriated them: "If one of the world's most successful oil companies can't do simple basic maintenance needed to keep the Prudhoe Bay field operating safely without interruption, maybe it shouldn't operate the pipeline," he fumed. "I am even more concerned about BP's corporate culture of seeming indifference to safety and environmental issues. And this comes from a company that prides itself in their ads on protecting the environment. *Shame, shame, shame.*"

Committee members grilled BP executives about why the company had failed to do adequate inspection and maintenance, and the BP executives solemnly promised to be more careful in the future. But no legislation was passed to force them to be. Four years later, BP spilled 210 million gallons of oil into the Gulf of Mexico from its Deepwater Horizon drilling rig, the worst oil spill in history.

If we're serious about restoring the common good, congressional shaming must be followed by legislation and criminal prosecutions that confirm the standard of behavior we expect. Such criminal investigations must be directed against individual wrongdoers rather than at companies as a whole. Corporations cannot feel shame; only individuals can. There is not much shame being associated with a large corporation that gets slapped with a fine. There can be a great deal of shame in personally going to jail. Yet these days few executives of major corporations and Wall Street banks are ever held personally accountable for illegal acts. As I've noted, no executive of any major bank was prosecuted for causing the 2008 financial crisis. This was not for lack of evidence. Goldman Sachs clearly misled its clients by betting against the same financial products it was peddling to them, to take but one example. Obama's Justice Department stopped bringing cases against corporate executives because, as ProPublica's Jesse Eisinger found, winning cases against individual executives has become too difficult and expensive for government prosecutors.

Corporations have become adept at giving their top

guns plausible deniability of knowledge in any nefarious scheme (Goldman executives used the abbreviation LDL—"let's discuss live"—to hide their traces), and prosecutors are routinely outgunned and outmaneuvered by platoons of high-priced corporate attorneys. Young government prosecutors who want lucrative partnerships in prestigious law firms when they leave government often don't want to jeopardize their career prospects, so they go easy on individual executives. They view the executives as "good people who have done one bad thing," as one SEC lawyer who was reluctant to bring charges against individual executives explained to Eisinger. It is often more convenient for prosecutors to give government a PR victory by slapping corporations with a fine (ultimately paid for by shareholders) and making them promise to behave better in the future. But individuals, not corporations, must be held accountable for undermining the common good. That is where the shame is. And shame is what is in short supply.

In recent years America has become confused about the difference between private morality and public morality. *Private* morality concerns what people do in private, often involving sex—sex between unmarried people or gay people, adultery, contraception, abortion, gay marriage, even which bathroom a transgendered person must use. *Public* morality involves what people do when they hold positions of power and public trust.

Some Americans object to women deciding to have an abortion, to gay people marrying, or to transgender people choosing a bathroom different from the gender on their birth certificate. I happen to believe intimate decisions like these should be left to these people rather than decided by government. But however you come out on private moral choices, there is little doubt that the nation is experiencing a significant crisis in *public* morality. When executives of pharmaceutical companies gouge consumers by jacking up the prices of drugs as high as possible; bank executives defraud their depositors by opening up sham accounts; and presidents denigrate the press, seem to endorse white supremacists, and disregard conflicts of financial interest, they are all engaging in acts of public immorality. They are rejecting the common good in favor of their own selfish needs for more wealth or power. This is shameful.

Some years ago William Bennett, scourge of personal immorality when and after he was secretary of education under Ronald Reagan, railed at Americans for being "less willing than we once were to sacrifice or to keep commitments." He said average people place a higher value than ever before on "personal growth, self-expression, and self-discovery." He accused the nation of adopting a "deeply ingrained philosophy that glorifies . . . freedom from constraints." Bennett's target was sexual license, but I think his words are more relevant to the whatever-it-takes creed that has overtaken American leadership. "Part of what it means to be a morally responsible human is to act in ways that are, sometimes, contrary to our 'natural' instincts," Bennett wrote. We struggle "against our bio-logical impulses, against our emotional longings. We do not abjure the struggle because it is difficult or because we seem to be battling against something deep within us . . . even if it seems fundamental to who we are."

In other words, using Bennett's logic but applying it to public rather than private morality, unconstrained desire for wealth and power is not to be excused just because it's part of human nature. All people—especially those who occupy positions of leadership and are entrusted with the well-being of many other people—should be held to a higher standard.

Respecting private morality does not, however, mean licensing sexual harassment and predation by the rich and powerful. That, too, is shameful. Yet society all too often ends up honoring such people while overlooking their abuses of power. In 2017 the Los Angeles Press Club honored movie mogul Harvey Weinstein by bestowing on him its Truthteller Award for Contributions to the Pub-lic Discourse and Cultural Enlightenment of Our Society. The organization called him an example of "integrity and social responsibility." While Weinstein distributed some laudable films, he also had a long history of harassing and abusing women in five-star hotel rooms. Apparently, this was an open secret in Hollywood. (Personal disclo-sure: Weinstein once distributed a film I co-created, but I did not know about his history of harassment until it was widely reported in October 2017.)

Why did Hollywood honor Weinstein despite this open

secret? In part because Weinstein raised money for many activities Hollywood approved of, including the presidential candidacy of Hillary Clinton. He also had the power to make and break careers, not just of starlets but also of an ecosystem of writers, journalists, and public relations specialists who directly or indirectly depended on him. As Rebecca Traister wrote in *New York* magazine's *The Cut,* "There were so many journalists on his payroll, working as consultants on movie projects, or as screenwriters, or for his magazine," that they shielded him from exposure and dared not sound the alarm. Shame on him, and shame on them.

Ideally, notions of right and wrong are sufficiently embedded in people's moral consciousness from an early age that they don't need to be honored or shamed into good behavior. The erosion of the common good over the past decades, however, suggests that such moral consciousness has waned. Society must buttress it, and in so doing remind others of acceptable limits. "Maintaining limits is a way of asserting community," sociologist James Q. Wilson has written. "If the limits are asserted weakly, uncertainly, or apologetically, their effects must certainly be weaker than if they are asserted boldly, confidently, and persuasively."

Setting limits isn't simply a matter of making and enforcing laws, because, as I have emphasized, clever lawyers can almost always find ways to skirt the letter of the law. When Donald Trump said he didn't pay taxes because he was "smart," he meant that his tax attorneys had found legal ways to circumvent the tax code. Setting the kind of limits society depends on requires public moral judgment. Just as we shouldn't be reluctant to celebrate behavior that exemplifies public morality, we shouldn't be reticent in condemning behavior that undermines it.

Faith-based leaders have a unique responsibility and opportunity here. Quite apart from whatever religious tenets they might hold or preach about private morality, they can help society distinguish private from public morality. They can also call for a public morality that rejects whatever-it-takes strategies for amassing personal wealth or power in favor of one that stresses our duties to one another. Moral guidance about what is right or decent can be found both in religious teachings and in our contemporary understanding of what we owe one another as members of the same society. As I have suggested, they overlap. A public morality that protects our democratic institutions, cherishes the truth, accepts our differences, ensures equal rights and equal opportunity, and invites passionate engagement in our civic life gives our own lives deeper meaning. It enlarges our capacities for attachment and love. It informs our sense of honor and shame. It equips us to be virtuous citizens.

America still bestows lots of honors and wields heaps of shame, but they're too often disconnected from the moral basis of society. If we're serious about reestablishing the moral foundation of our life together, we must change how and whom we honor or shame, and reconnect these practices to the good we hold in common. And what we do in our own society should be a guide for what we do in the world.

CHAPTER 9

Resurrecting Truth

REVIVING THE COMMON GOOD also depends on each of us taking responsibility for finding, sharing, and insisting upon public truth. By public truth I mean facts about what is happening around us that could affect our well-being, as well as clear logic about the significance of those facts and reasoned analysis about their practical consequences.

Particular people have special responsibilities in this regard. We rely on scientists, researchers, professors, analysts, and journalists—in laboratories, universities, think tanks, government agencies, and in the media—to discover and report the truth. We depend on leaders of business, government, and nonprofits to relay the truth. We need fact-checkers, truth-tellers, whistle-blowers, and investigative reporters to help us uncover the truth when we've been lied to.

But in recent years, the tendency to do whatever it takes to gain wealth or power has undermined truth, and called into question all these roles and responsibilities. Even before Donald Trump became president, comedian Stephen Colbert joked that the statements of politicians only approximated the truth—"truthiness," as he called it. The mainstream media, for their part, have occasionally slanted the news out of fear of offending major advertisers or powerful interests in government. *New York Times* reporter Judith Miller notoriously colluded with the George W. Bush administration in propagating its blatant lie about Saddam Hussein's supposed weapons of mass destruction. Meanwhile, journalists have been under mounting pressure to deliver stories that attract the largest number of viewers or readers rather than inform readers and viewers of important truths. Corporate public relations professionals, who now vastly outnumber professional journalists, do whatever it takes to get favorable stories for their companies and avoid unfavorable ones. Because of ever-intensifying competition for funding, universities and nonprofit research institutions sometimes shape their research agendas to satisfy funders; some even suppress analyses that funders dislike.

All of this paved the way for Trump—his ubiquitous lies, his ongoing attacks on journalists, and his assault on scientists and researchers. They also served as a prelude to "fake news," some of it coming from foreign sources intent on undermining trust in our democracy.

We must not normalize public lying. The common good requires vigilance against it, and the summoning of public shame when we find it. It is a central obligation of politicians as well as journalists, researchers, scientists, and academicians to inform the public of the truth, and to identify lies without fear of retribution. It is the civic responsibility of all of us to check the facts we read or hear, to find and depend upon reliable sources, to share the truth with others, and hold accountable those who lie to us or suppress the truth.

We must also ensure that every American has sufficient education to differentiate truth from falsehood, and to think critically about what they read and see. As I'll explain shortly, public education is not just a private investment; it's a public good. Yet that good is eroding. In 2016, one out of every four Americans believed the sun rotates around the earth; a third did not believe in evolution; a third did not accept the reality of global warming, and even among those who did, many did not believe humans are at least partly responsible. Without a shared truth, democratic deliberation is impossible.

The only way we can understand the true dimensions of the problems we face together is with accurate facts about them from sources the public trusts, along with logical assessment of those facts. As Daniel Patrick Moynihan once said, everyone is entitled to their own opinions but not their own facts. He might have added that everyone is entitled to their own interpretations but not their own logic. When we accept lies as facts, or illogic as logic, we lose the shared reality necessary to tackle our common problems. We become powerless.

The challenge of reviving trust in the sources of truth is especially difficult in an era of raging inequality, when big money can suppress truth and buy off criticism. Our democracy is directly imperiled when the rich buy off politicians but no less endangered when the rich buy off the institutions our democracy depends on to research, investigate, expose, and mobilize action against what is occurring. David Koch's $23 million of donations to public television earned him positions on the boards of two prominent public broadcasting stations. These positions also helped ensure that a documentary critical of Koch and his brother Charles, called *Citizen Koch,* did not air on public television. The documentary, about the secretive political spending by the Koch brothers as well as other wealthy individuals, was to be broadcast on PBS stations nationwide. Its funding was abruptly cut off when, it appears, Koch was offended by it.

Or consider Google's financial power to marshal the facts it wants the public to know, and suppress those it doesn't. Some background: Google's search engine runs two-thirds of all searches in the United States and 90 percent in Europe. Such a "platform monopoly" can squelch innovation if, for example, Google favored in searches its own services, such as Google Maps and Google Shopping—which is one reason why the European Commission hit Google with a record €2.42 billion fine in June 2017. Why hasn't Google run into similar problems with antitrust authorities in the United States? It almost did in 2012 when the Federal Trade Commission's Bureau of Competition recommended that the commission sue

Google for conduct that "has resulted—and will result—in real harm to . . . innovation." The commissioners decided not to pursue the case, and gave no explanation for their decision. As a former official of the commission, I can tell you it's highly unusual for the commissioners to decide against a staff recommendation without comment. Their decision may have had to do with Google's political clout. Google is among the largest corporate lobbyists in the United States and a major campaign donor to Democrats, who then controlled the White House and the Senate.

Google also has enough financial power to stifle criticism coming from independent researchers. In September 2017, *The New York Times* reported that the New America Foundation, an influential center-left think tank, fired researcher Barry Lynn, a sharp critic of platform monopolies like Google's. Lynn had posted a congratulatory note to European officials on their Google decision, and called for American antitrust officials to follow suit. Since its founding in 1999, the New America Foundation had received more than $21 million from Google (and its parent company, Alphabet) and from the family foundation of Eric Schmidt, the executive chairman of Alphabet who previously served as chairman of New America's board. According to the *Times,* Schmidt didn't like Lynn's comments and communicated his displeasure to the president of the New America Foundation. She then accused Lynn of "imperiling the institution as a whole," and fired him and his staff. What really imperils the New America Foundation is firings such as this one, which distort its mission and undermine its credibility.

Google also pays off academics to help sway public opinion and policymakers in its favor. In late 2017, *The Wall Street Journal* reported that Google has quietly financed hundreds of professors at universities such as Harvard and Berkeley to write research papers that help Google defend itself against regulatory challenges to its market dominance, paying $5,000 to $400,000 on a wish list of topics. Google has used the resulting research in courtrooms, regulatory hearings, and congressional hearings. Some professors have allowed Google to see the papers before they're published, enabling Google to offer "suggestions," according to emails obtained by the *Journal.* The professors' research papers do not disclose that Google sought them out, and don't necessarily reveal Google's backing.

Trump's shoot-the-messenger war on truth-telling institutions has been an extension of all this. When opinion polls have shown Trump with low approval ratings, he has attacked the polling industry, asserting that "any negative polls are fake news." When government researchers and scientists have come up with facts that contradict positions Trump has taken, he has criticized the researchers and scientists. When, as a candidate, Trump didn't like the positive employment numbers from the Bureau of Labor Statistics showing the economy improving under the Obama administration, he called the official unemployment rate "a phony number." When the nonpartisan Congressional Budget Office estimated that large numbers of Americans would lose their health insurance coverage as a result of the plan the Republicans were then promoting to repeal the Affordable Care Act, Trump's press secretary warned that the Congressional Budget Office could not be trusted to come up with accurate numbers. When Trump disagreed with a judicial finding that his original travel ban was intended to prevent Muslims from entering the United States, he called the judge who made the finding a "so-called judge" and attacked the appellate judges who upheld it as "so political" they weren't "able to read a statement and do what's right."

Trump and his administration have drummed up evidence to support positions they want to take, suppressed government data that doesn't back up their positions, and removed fact-finders who won't cooperate. When Trump couldn't find evidence to support his claim that "three to five million" fraudulent votes were cast for Hillary Clinton in the 2016 election, he created a commission to find such evidence. When the academic members of the Environmental Protection Agency's Board of Scientific Counselors, the outside advisory committee that reviews the work of scientists within the agency, found that climate change was a reality, the EPA did not renew their membership. An EPA spokesman said they would be replaced by industry "experts" who better "understand the impact of regulations on the regulated community." In September 2017, the Treasury Department removed from its website a 2012 economic analysis showing that when corporations are taxed, only a small portion of the tax's final cost is paid by workers while most falls on shareholders. The analysis contradicted Treasury Secretary Steven Mnuchin's argument that a corporate tax cut would mostly benefit workers. A spokeswoman from the department explained "the paper was a dated staff analysis from the previous administration. It does not represent our current thinking and analysis." Several weeks after Hurricane Maria devastated Puerto Rico, as Trump tweeted that the federal government was doing "a GREAT job" restoring the island, the Federal Emergency Management Agency removed data from its website showing that half of Puerto Ricans still did not have access to drinking water and only 5 percent had electricity.

We cannot be effective citizens in a democracy if truths unfavorable to those with power are suppressed, while lies favorable to them are offered as truth. If a cabinet secretary finds fault with an analysis done by a prior administration, he or she has a responsibility to explain to the public what those faults are. If an agency removes data that had been available to the public, the agency must explain why. Political leaders who disparage legitimate truth-telling institutions or hide the truth from the public are committing acts of intellectual treason. They are undermining our democracy. Perpetrators must be revealed and shamed.

The same standard of truth-telling must apply to the private and nonprofit sectors, and to universities. Think tanks that suppress research their funders don't like should no longer be entitled to a tax exemption, and their subsequent research reports should give notice that they selectively report the truth. Academics who accept money from corporations or other groups with financial stakes in the outcomes of their research must disclose the sources of their funding in all their resulting papers and in all subsequent testimony. Universities must not accept any funding that restricts the range of research they do.

Guarding the freedom and independence of the press is also essential to maintaining truth as a common good. As Thomas Jefferson wrote from Paris to Edward Carrington, whom Jefferson sent as a delegate to the Continental Congress from 1786 to 1788, the best way to ensure a responsive government is to give citizens "full information of their affairs thro' the channel of the public papers, & to contrive that those papers should penetrate the whole mass of the people. . . . Were it left to me to decide whether we should have a government without newspapers or newspapers without a government, I should not hesitate a moment to prefer the latter. But I should mean that every man should receive those papers & be capable of reading them."

Yet 230 years later, the press's freedom and independence are under siege, and a growing segment of the public no longer trusts the major media. Distrust was on the rise even before Trump. On the eve of the 2016 presidential election, only 18 percent of Americans said they trusted national news media, according to the Pew Research Center. In a Gallup poll at about the same time, nearly two-thirds of Americans believed the mainstream press was filled with "fake news." Contrast this with American opinion almost five decades before. In 1972, in the wake of investigative reporting that revealed truths about Vietnam and Nixon's Watergate scandal, 72 percent of Americans expressed trust and confidence in the press.

The precipitous decline can be attributed partly to the media's increasing willingness to do whatever it takes to maximize profits. Most large media corporations are moved by shareholder returns, not the common good. In order to generate high profits and share prices, they have to attract consumers rather than serve citizens. This has transformed journalists from investigators and analysts offering serious news to "content providers" competing for attention. Broadcast media are obsessed by ratings. A Harvard study found that in the 2008 presidential election the major TV networks devoted a total of 220 minutes to reporting candidates' positions on issues of public policy; four years later, the networks allocated 114 minutes to policy; in 2016, they devoted 32 minutes. Hillary Clinton's policy ideas and proposals received almost no attention while her emails commanded 100 minutes of airtime. Meanwhile, Donald Trump's antics ruled the airwaves. His eagerness to vilify, disparage, denounce, and defame others—not just Clinton but also President Obama, Mexican Americans, Muslims, new immigrants, other nations (especially China), Democrats, other Republicans, and the press—turned him into a magnet for readers and viewers, and not just on Fox News. Regardless of whether they were appalled or thrilled by his diatribes, they were entertained.

Schooled in reality television and New York tabloids, Trump has known how to drive ratings. Notwithstanding his attacks on the media, top media executives have been delighted. As the 2016 presidential race heated up, Leslie Moonves, CEO of CBS, said the Trump phenomenon "may not be good for America, but it's damn good for CBS," adding, "Who would have expected the ride we're all having right now? The money's rolling in and this is fun.... I've never seen anything like this, and this is going to be a very good year for us. Sorry. It's a terrible thing to say. But, bring it on, Donald. Keep going." No wonder Trump received more coverage than any presidential candidate in American history. As president, he has continued to dominate the news, for much the same reasons.

Moonves knew his admission was "a terrible thing to say" because he was aware that the common good required a different response, and probably less coverage of Trump. The Communications Act of 1934, which continues to be the charter for broadcast television, recognizes its responsibility to the common good—requiring that licensees serve "the public interest, convenience and necessity." I wouldn't want government to intrude on CBS News's editorial judgment about how much to cover Trump or any other candidate, but the act signals that CBS and the other major networks have a responsibility to the public that transcends their ratings. At the least, network news divisions should be independent of top executives who represent the interests of shareholders. This was the case before the 1980s—before the corporate transformation I outlined—when the news divisions of America's three major broadcast networks made decisions based not on how much profit they generated but on what an informed public needed to know. Former CBS correspondent Marvin Kalb remembers CBS's owner and chairman William Paley telling news reporters in the 1960s, "I have Jack Benny to make money." Now, however, the owners and major investors in broadcast television demand that their news divisions make money.

This evolution paved the way not only for Trump's dominance of the news cycle after becoming president, but also his ongoing assaults on journalists—"the most dishonest human beings on earth," as he has called them, "the lowest forms of life," "scum," "sick," purveyors of "fake news," and the "enemy of the people," even suggesting that their goal was to remove him from office (they "have their own agenda, and it's not your agenda, and it's not the country's agenda"). The harangues have scored points with Trump's base and served to discredit anything the press discovers that could damage him, but at the expense of a weakened democracy. If a large enough portion of the public comes to trust Trump's words more than they do the media's, Trump can get away with saying—and doing— whatever he wants. When that happens, democracy ends.

The debasement of the press has sometimes led to violence. On the eve of his election to the House of Representatives, Montana Republican candidate Greg Gianforte beat up Ben Jacobs, a reporter for the *Guardian* newspaper. The violence was prompted by Jacobs asking Gianforte for his reaction to the Congressional Budget Office's report showing that the House Republican substitute for the Affordable Care Act would result in 23 million Americans losing their health insurance. At that point, in the words of a Fox News team member who witnessed the attack: "Gianforte grabbed Jacobs by the neck with both hands and slammed him into the ground behind him. . . . Gianforte then began punching the reporter. As Gianforte moved on top of Jacobs, he began yelling something to the effect of, 'I'm sick and tired of this!' Jacobs scrambled to his knees and said something about his glasses being broken. . . . To be clear, at no point did any of us who witnessed this assault see Jacobs show any form of physical aggression toward Gianforte, who left the area after giving statements to local sheriff's deputies."

Gianforte's attack on Jacobs was shameful enough. Almost as shameful was Gianforte's press release about what occurred, which blamed Jacobs. "It's unfortunate that this aggressive behavior from a liberal journalist created this scene at our campaign volunteer BBQ." It was a blatant lie, as evinced by the Fox News team and the charge against Gianforte. Under Trump, though, blatant lying has become the new normal, and a "liberal journalist" the enemy. Gianforte was elected and allowed to take his seat in Congress. He is now known as "the honorable" Greg Gianforte, but there is nothing honorable about his behavior. Kathleen Hall Jamieson, director of the Annenberg Public Policy Center at the University of Pennsylvania, said that Trump "has contributed to a climate of discourse consistent with assaulting a reporter for asking an inconvenient question." Whether you agree or disagree with Donald Trump's policies, all of us must stand up against this. It is the road to despotism.

Even had there been no disparaging comments or threats by Trump and other politicians, the media would still need to rebuild public trust. Print and broadcast news outlets must demonstrate to the public that their news stories are produced accurately and intelligently. They need codes of ethics with clearly stated processes for checking facts and correcting errors, and ways to ensure that the public is made aware of such corrections. They must clearly separate facts and analysis from opinions and advocacy, and inform readers and viewers of any news or news-gathering that is funded by organizations with a stake in what's reported. They need ombudsmen to investigate public complaints about their coverage, along with public editors who serve as paid in-house critics. These steps are necessary not only to rebuild public trust, but also to restore the media to its rightful place in our democracy and protect the truth as a common good.

At one time I believed that social media would democratize the news—enabling more people to become truth-tellers, give more of us access to a greater range of stories and perspectives, and provide a useful alternative to corporate media. I was wrong. Instead, social media has enshrouded all of us in cocoons of our own making. We are too easily tyrannized by algorithms that feed us only the facts, analyses, and opinions we already favor. We no longer live in a common reality but, rather, a reality shared only with those who already agree with us. (We're also clustering geographically, choosing to live around people who share our values. In 2016, eight out of ten U.S. counties voted overwhelmingly for either Donald Trump or Hillary Clinton.)

I believe it is our responsibility to break out of these self-generated bubbles. We need to seek alternative sources of news and information that don't merely confirm our biases and preconceptions, and test our views by seeking out people with different views and opinions. I'm sure I still remain largely in my own bubble, but I make an effort to break out. I read daily editorials and comments in *The Wall Street Journal* as well as *The New York Times;* the *National Review* as well as *The American Prospect; The Weekly Standard* and *The Nation.* I try to make a point of exchanging views with conservatives and Republicans. I almost always accept speaking invitations from universities in red states. I still have a long way to go. But I sincerely believe—and I tell my students—that the best way to learn anything is to talk with someone who disagrees with you.

The ease with which just about anyone can post anything on the Internet and gain a following poses another danger to the truth. All you need is a smartphone to photograph or video in real time, and you can create your own fake virtual newsroom. With a bit more effort you can spread lies to millions of people by using algorithm-friendly headlines and search-optimized "keyword bombs." You can deploy millions of bots to move a fake news article to the top of Facebook Trending Topics or Google search. If you can afford it, you can hire a data-mining firm to discover and aggregate personal information on tens of millions of people—uncovering their concerns and biases—thereby enabling you to give them custom-tailored "news" and ads designed to exploit these emotions. In this new world, truth can be doctored to meet anyone's needs. According to *BuzzFeed*, during the final three months of the 2016 presidential campaign the top-performing fake election news stories on Facebook generated more engagement than the top stories from major news outlets such as *The New York Times, The Washington Post, The Huffington Post,* and NBC News.

The dilemma is how to police against this, and whom to trust with the policing. Should we give Facebook, Google, and giant servers like Cloudflare the responsibility? Or should we expect the government to assume this role? In a free society, where exactly is the border between fake news and dissent, and who should decide? I don't have any simple answers to these questions, but here, too, I think each of us has a critical role to play. We have a responsibility to educate ourselves and others about how to find the truth, and how to assess the news we receive thoughtfully and critically. We need to learn better how to recognize lies so we can refrain from sharing them and warn others. We need to demand that the leaders of news-gathering organizations—not just print and broadcast media, but also giant tech companies like Facebook, Google, and Twitter—

understand their role as trustees of the common good, and take appropriate steps to guard the truth. As I've said, we should honor truth-tellers—whistle-blowers, investigative reporters, and courageous public servants who tell us what we need to know rather than what we want to know. And we should shame the liars and truth-suppressors—those who use their wealth, power, and positions of authority to mislead the public.

We should also prevent data-mining bots from exploiting our private biases and concerns—as revealed on the Internet—to flood us with custom-tailored news and ads. The way to do this is to make our personal information private. There is no good reason why data about everything we view or buy on the Internet, as well as everything we read or see and where we travel, should be available to anyone other than ourselves. This information is not a common good. To the contrary, it is private. But to make it private, we will need a law that prevents Facebook, Google, data-mining firms, and other potential aggregators of personal information from using it. As citizens, I believe we have an obligation to push for such a law.

CHAPTER 10

Civic Education for All

FINALLY, AND NOT LEAST, restoring the common good requires a new commitment to civic education—as part of the formal education of children and young people, as well as the ongoing education of us all. Our children need to understand themselves not just as individuals seeking self-expression and lucrative careers but also as citizens responsible for upholding our core common values. They need to learn to respect but also reform the major institutions of our society. They should be equipped to deliberate with others over what is best for our society and the world, and to civilly and respectfully disagree.

When I heard John F. Kennedy's adjuration that we ask what we can do for our nation, I was attending a small public high school in upstate New York. Part of the required curriculum was called "citizenship education." It involved a series of courses on history and government. As in most schools, some were well taught while others were taught abysmally. I remember one teacher who often pointed to a world map showing the Soviet Union, China, and most of Eastern Europe in bright red, with surrounding nations in pink. Her ongoing civics lesson was that communism was spreading like an infectious disease. If we weren't careful, what remained of the free world would catch it. Civic education in the 1950s reflected many of the prejudices of the day. Yet it at least engaged us, day after day, in the practice of thinking about the well-being of our society and the world. The ongoing examination of history and our system of government had a cumulative effect: Regardless of our politics, we began to see ourselves as the inheritors of an important legacy. That legacy was far from perfect, but it was profoundly important. We had an obligation to become responsible citizens.

Civic education was long ago eliminated from the standard high school curriculum. In its place has come a narrowed focus on English and math, along with an avalanche of tests. At the same time, higher education has become ever more vocational. Students crowd into courses on economics and business, or computer engineering. All told, education is now viewed mainly as a private investment rather than a public good.

This is understandable. As I've noted, with inequalities of income and wealth wider than they have been in over a century, parents and their children face the daunting possibilities of unprecedented riches for those with the "right" education, or squalor for those on the losing track. What you learn is what you'll earn, as the popular saying goes. Over his or her lifetime the typical high school dropout will accumulate no more than half the earnings of a high school graduate, while the typical college graduate will earn twice as much as someone with only a high school degree. Yet if education is simply a private investment yielding private returns, there is no reason why anyone other than the "investor" should pay for it. No wonder increasing numbers of parents resist paying for the education of other children, especially those who are poorer or require extra teacher time and resources. The same attitude extends to legislatures that have been cutting funding for public universities. If a university degree is a private investment offering a good return to the individual, they argue, why should taxpayers bear the cost? It would seem more appropriate for students and their parents to take out loans to cover it, just as people borrow for all sorts of other worthwhile investments, such as a new home or business.

Education, though, is not just a private investment. It is also a public good. America's founding fathers understood that our democracy depends on it. As historian Alan Taylor has observed, they knew emperors and kings could easily mislead uneducated publics. The survival of the founders' new republic necessitated a public wise enough to keep power within bounds. It required citizens capable of resolving the tension between private interests and the common good—people imbued, in the language of the time, with civic virtue.

At the close of the Constitutional Convention of 1787, a woman was said to have asked Benjamin Franklin what sort of government the delegates had created for the people. He replied, "A republic, if you can keep it." What did "keeping it" require? More than anything else, education. "Ignorance and despotism seem made for each other," Jefferson warned. But if the new nation could "enlighten the people generally . . . tyranny and the oppressions of mind and body will vanish, like evil spirits at the dawn of day." During the colonial era a few towns ran public grammar schools—but only for a few weeks in the winter when family farms didn't require their children's labor. Other towns relied on private tuition. After the Revolution, reformers pushed for free public education. Jedediah Peck of upstate New York typified the reform movement. "In all countries where education is confined to a few people," he warned, "we always find arbitrary governments and abject slavery." Peck persuaded the New York legislature to create a comprehensive system of public education.

The person most credited with founding American public schooling, Massachusetts educator Horace Mann, also linked public education to democracy. "A republican form of government, without intelligence in the people," he wrote, "must be, on a vast scale, what a mad-house, without superintendent or keepers, would be on a small one." Mann believed it important that public schools educate all children together, "in common." The mix of ethnicities, races, and social classes in the same schools would help children learn the habits and attitudes of citizenship. (His project was not without fault: It emphasized Protestantism over Catholicism, for example, which was one reason Catholics created their own private schools.) The goal of inculcating public morality extended through higher education as well. Charles W. Eliot, who became president of Harvard in 1869, believed "the best solution to the problem of national order lay in the education of individuals to the ideals of service, stewardship, and cooperation."

If the common good is to be restored, education must be reconnected to these public moral roots. We must stop thinking about it solely as a private investment that may lead to a good-paying job, and revive the founders' understanding of it as a public good that helps train young people in responsible citizenship. This requires that schools focus not just on building skills but also on teaching civic obligations. For starters, every child should gain an understanding of our political system, the Constitution, the Bill of Rights, separation of powers, checks and balances, and federalism. They must understand the meaning and importance of the rule of law, and why no one should be above it, and they need to know where these legacies came from, and why they continue to be important. This is what we demand of people who want to become naturalized citizens: Immigrants have to pass a civics test covering the organization of the U.S. government and American history. When I served as secretary of labor I had the privilege of administering the Pledge of Allegiance to some of those who had passed that test, and witnessed their pride and gratitude in being welcomed into citizenship.

Every child must also understand the difference between how our system *should* work and how it *actually* works, and why we all have an obligation to seek to bridge that gap. Which means they must grasp the meaning and importance of justice—of equal political rights and equal economic opportunity, and how these two goals are related. They need to see how the economy is organized, how its rules are made, and what groups and interests have the most influence in making those rules. They must learn to be open to new thoughts and ideas, and practice tolerance toward different beliefs, ethnicities, races, and religions. They need to learn about basic human rights, and America's responsibilities in the world. As political philosopher Martha Nussbaum has suggested, students should learn not only that citizens of India have equal basic human rights, for example, but also about the problems of hunger and pollution in India and the implications of these problems for the larger issues of global hunger and global ecology.

Civic education must instill in young people a passion for truth. It should enable them to think critically, be skeptical (but not cynical) about what they hear and read, find reliable sources of information, apply basic logic and analysis, and know enough about history and the physical world to differentiate fact from fiction. They need to understand how important the truth is to democracy, and to our capacity to deliberate together about the common good.

Such an education must, finally, encourage civic virtue. It should explain and illustrate the profound differences between doing whatever it takes to win and acting for the common good; between getting as much as one can get for oneself and giving back to society; between assuming everyone is in it for themselves and understanding that we're all in it together; between seeking personal celebrity, wealth, or power and helping to build a better society for all. An education in civic virtue should explain why the latter choices are morally necessary.

Such an education must also urge and equip young people to communicate with others who do not share their views. It should teach them how to listen, to open their minds to the possibility that their own views and pre-conceptions may be wrong, and to discover why people with opposing views believe what they do. It should enable them to work with others to separate facts and logic from values and beliefs, and help them find facts and apply logic together even if their values and beliefs differ.

These lessons cannot be learned only in the classroom. A true civic education also requires learning by doing. Young people must develop the "habits of the heart," as Tocqueville called them, by taking on responsibilities in their communities—working in homeless shelters and soup kitchens, tutoring, mentoring, coaching kids' sports teams, helping the elderly and infirm. Young people need to move out of their bubbles of class, race, religion, and ideology, and to go to places and engage in activities where people look different from themselves, and have different beliefs and outlooks from their own. They must learn to communicate with them. They need to learn how to *learn* from them.

Two years of required public service would give young

people an opportunity to learn civic responsibility by serving the common good directly. It should be a duty of citizenship. This is how we once regarded military service. From World War II until the final days of the Vietnam War, in January 1973, nearly every young man in America faced the prospect of being drafted. Sure, many children of the rich found means to stay out of harm's way, but the draft at least spread responsibility and heightened the public's sensitivity to the human costs of war. Richard Nixon officially ended the draft and created a paid military mainly to take the wind out of the sails of the antiwar movement, and he succeeded.

Since then, the United States has had what's called an "all-volunteer" army—"volunteer" only in the sense that for some young people these jobs are the best they can get. Today's military is composed of fewer young people from rich families than the population as a whole. When compared with other groups of the same age, the military also has more Southerners and a higher percentage of African Americans. Most come from the same kind of blue-collar households whose incomes have gone nowhere for four decades. It's easy to support a war that you don't have to fight in. A 2004 survey showed that the majority of young people supported the U.S. invasion of Iraq but only a small minority were themselves willing to fight in that war.

Two years in the armed services or in some other service to the nation would help instill in all young people a sense of their obligations to society, regardless of their family's wealth or status. It would allow young Americans to connect with other Americans who differ from them by race, social class, and politics. Not incidentally, it might also remind many upper-income Americans of the personal costs and risks of American foreign policy.

Public service could take many forms in addition to military service. The Peace Corps could be revived and expanded. Projects like Teach For America could be enlarged and extended to other service professions, like Social Work for America. Nonprofits could offer a range of public service work. All such recruits would be paid a modest stipend, at least living expenses plus interest payments on any student loans. That would be less than the current pay of "all-volunteer" army recruits.

Whenever the idea of national service comes up, some object that no one should be forced to serve their country. In 2003, when George W. Bush proposed expanding AmeriCorps, the editorial board of *The Wall Street Journal* grumbled that "the entire concept of paid volunteerism is an oxymoron." Dick Armey, then House majority leader, opined, "We give least well when we give at the direction and supervision of the government. The idea that government can teach charity to America rings very hollow with me."

Rubbish. Young people were forced to serve their country when we had a draft. We require children to attend school for sixteen years in order to learn the basics. Why shouldn't they be required to put in two years of public service, to help learn the basics of citizenship? Besides, national service has nothing whatever to do with government teaching "charity." It is about teaching civic virtue. Universities could also devote the second semester of the junior year to public service. This wouldn't be a break from a student's education but an inherent part of it.

Once learned, civic virtue must be practiced. As I hope I've made clear, our obligations as citizens go beyond voting, paying taxes, obeying the law, and serving on juries. We owe to one another our time and energies to improve our communities and to protect and strengthen our democracy. This should not be thought of as "charity," either. It is a commitment to pass on to future generations a society that comes closer to its ideals than it was when it was passed on to us.

I've noted that a majority of today's Americans worry that the nation is losing its national identity. If you examine our history, you'll see that the core of that identity has not been the whiteness of our skin or the uniformity of our ethnicity. It has been the ideals we share, the good we have held in common. If we are losing our national identity, it is not because we come in more colors or speak more languages than before. It is because we are losing our sense of common good. This is what must be restored.

That common good, as I have emphasized, is a set of shared commitments—to the rule of law, and to the spirit as well as the letter of the law; to our democratic institutions of government; to truth; to tolerance of our differences; to equal political rights and equal opportunity; to participating in our civic life, and making necessary sacrifices for the ideals we hold in common. We must share these commitments if we are to have a functioning society. They inform our judgments about right and wrong because they constitute our common good. Without them, there is no "we."

Whether that common good can be recovered will depend in part on establishing a new ethic of leadership based on trusteeship; an appropriate application of honor and shame; a renewed commitment to truth; and a dedication to the civic education of our children and ourselves, about the obligations we owe one another as citizens.

Some of you may feel such a quest to be hopeless. The era we are living in offers too many illustrations of greed, narcissism, and hatefulness. I, however, firmly believe it is not hopeless. Almost every day I witness or hear of the compassion and generosity of ordinary Americans. Their actions rarely make headlines, but they constitute much of our daily life together. The challenge is to turn all this into a new public spiritedness extending to the highest reaches in the land—a public morality that strengthens our democracy, makes our economy work for everyone, and revives trust in the major institutions of America.

The moral fiber of our society has been weakened, but it has not been destroyed. We can recover the rule of law and preserve our democratic institutions by taking a more active role in politics. We can protect the truth by using facts and logic to combat lies. We can fight against all forms of bigotry. We can strengthen the bonds that connect us to one another by reaching out, and help resurrect civility by acting more civilly toward those with whom we disagree.

We have never been a perfect union. Our finest moments have been when we sought to become more perfect than we had been. We can help restore the common good by striving for it and showing others it's worth the effort. I worked for Robert F. Kennedy a half century ago when the common good was well understood. Resurrecting it may take another half century, or more. But as the theologian Reinhold Niebuhr once said, "Nothing that is worth doing can be achieved in our lifetime; therefore we must be saved by hope. Nothing which is true or beautiful or good makes complete sense in any immediate context of history."

Acknowledgments

This book is the product of many conversations over the years with friends and associates too numerous to mention, but I owe special thanks to Harley Shaiken, Sasha Leitman, Andrew Santana, Mark Lilla, Adam Reich, and Aarin Walker. I am particularly indebted to my friend and editor for over thirty-five years, Jonathan Segal, who urged me to write this book, and to my wife, Perian Flaherty, who gave me the courage to do so.

Recommended Reading

The following list comprises my nominees for a basic curriculum in civic education. They're documents, books (both nonfiction and fiction), speeches, a few poems, and even one film, all of which I believe to be particularly helpful in understanding the common good in America, and what it requires of us.

The Declaration of Independence (1776)
The Constitution of the United States (1787)
The Bill of Rights (1791)
The Fourteenth Amendment to the Constitution (1868)

. . .

Maya Angelou, "On the Pulse of Morning" (1993)
Hannah Arendt, *The Origins of Totalitarianism* (1951)
Black Hawk, Surrender speech (1832)
Brown v. Board of Education, U.S. Supreme Court (1954)
Dee Brown, *Bury My Heart at Wounded Knee* (1970)
Edmund Burke, *Reflections on the Revolution in France* (1790)
Edmund Burke, "Thoughts on the Cause of the Present
    Discontents" (1770)
Frank Capra, screenplay for *It's a Wonderful Life* (1946)

Rachel Carson, *Silent Spring* (1962)

Censure of Senator Joseph McCarthy (1954)

Herbert Croly, *The Promise of American Life* (1909)

Dred Scott v. Sandford, U.S. Supreme Court (1857)

Ralph Ellison, *Invisible Man* (1952)

Ralph Waldo Emerson, "Self-Reliance" (1841)

Gideon v. Wainwright, U.S. Supreme Court (1963)

Woody Guthrie, "This Land Is Your Land" (1944)

Alexander Hamilton, John Jay, James Madison, *The Federalist Papers* (1787–88)

Václav Havel, "The Power of the Powerless" (1978)

Joseph Heller, *Catch-22* (1961)

Langston Hughes, "Let America Be America Again" (1935)

Thomas Jefferson, First Inaugural Address (1801)

John F. Kennedy, Inaugural Address (1961)

Martin Luther King, Jr., "I Have a Dream" speech (1963)

Martin Luther King, Jr., Speech at the Great March on Detroit (1963)

Emma Lazarus, "The New Colossus" (1883)

Abraham Lincoln, Springfield Lyceum speech (1838)

Abraham Lincoln, "A House Divided" speech (1858)

Abraham Lincoln, First Inaugural Address (1861)

Abraham Lincoln, Gettysburg Address (1863)

Abraham Lincoln, Emancipation Proclamation (1863)

James Madison, Letter to Thomas Jefferson (February 4, 1790)

Marbury v. Madison, U.S. Supreme Court (1803)

McCulloch v. Maryland, U.S. Supreme Court (1819)

Montesquieu, *The Spirit of the Laws* (1748)

George Orwell, "Notes on Nationalism" (1945)

George Orwell, "Politics and the English Language" (1946)

Thomas Paine, *Common Sense* (1776)

Thomas Paine, *Rights of Man* (1791)

Karl Popper, *The Open Society and Its Enemies* (1945)

John Rawls, "Justice as Fairness" (1985)

Franklin D. Roosevelt, State of the Union Address ("The Four Freedoms") (1941)

Theodore Roosevelt, "The New Nationalism" (1910)
Seneca Falls Declaration (1848)
David Simon, *The Wire,* TV series (2002–08)
John Steinbeck, *The Grapes of Wrath* (1939)
Henry David Thoreau, "Resistance to Civil Government" (1849)
Alexis de Tocqueville, *Democracy in America* (1835, 1840)
Virginia Statute for Religious Freedom (1786)
George Washington, Farewell Address (1796)
Walt Whitman, *Leaves of Grass* (1855)
John Winthrop, "A Model of Christian Charity" (1630)

A Discussion Guide for

The Common Good

I hope this book will encourage you to get together with others to discuss the common good. The following questions might guide such a discussion.

PART I What Is the Common Good?

1. How do you define "the common good" in America? What do Americans have in common other than national symbols like the flag and the national anthem? What do these symbols mean to you?
2. Do Americans have obligations to the nation in addition to paying taxes, serving on juries, and voting? If so, what are they?
3. Some say Americans are selfish and self-centered. Others point to acts of kindness and courage—first responders to emergencies, everyday acts of altruism. How would you describe our national character?
4. Has America's character changed over time—since your parents were children, for example? If so, how and why?
5. Do you trust government to do the right thing most of the time? Do you believe in our *system* of government—the

Constitution, the Bill of Rights, federalism, and the rule of law?

6. What's the difference between a concern for the common good and nationalism?

7. What role does a president play in setting the moral tone of the nation?

PART II What Happened to the Common Good?

8. Why has the public's trust in all major American institutions—especially government, big businesses, banks, and the media—plunged over the past forty years? What events or trends have been most responsible for the decline?

9. Americans appear to have become far more partisan than we were forty years ago—liberals have moved to the "left" and conservatives to the "right," Republicans and Democrats are less willing to compromise, and everyone seems to be angrier. Why has this happened?

10. Have widening inequalities of income and wealth played a part?

11. Has the flood of big money into our political system played a part?

12. Are the two related?

13. Why before the 1980s did big corporations have responsibilities toward their communities and their workers, in addition to their shareholders? Why after the 1980s did big corporations focus solely on maximizing profits and shareholder returns? Should corporations go back to their former ways?

14. A major theme in the 2016 presidential election, coming from both major parties, was that the economic system is "rigged" for the benefit of those at the top. Why did this theme appear so prominently in 2016 and not before? Do you agree with it?

PART III Can the Common Good Be Restored?

15. What are the attributes of good leadership? Do leaders of business, government, and the media have responsibilities to restore trust in their institutions? If so, how should they go about it?

16. What roles do honor and shame play in contemporary American society? Ideally, who should be honored and for what, and who should be shamed and for what? How should such honoring and shaming occur?

17. Who do you trust to inform you about public issues such as climate change, the economy, or dangers posed by foreign governments? What are the qualities or characteristics you look for in deciding whom to trust in conveying the truth?

18. Does a democracy depend on a shared reality, or can a democracy function with people believing fundamentally different facts?

19. Are Americans adequately educated about how government and the economy are supposed to work, as well as how they actually work? If not, what should that education consist of, and when should it begin?

20. Do Americans have sufficient understanding of the obligations of citizenship? If not, who should be responsible for providing this understanding? Parents? Teachers? Public officials?

21. Do we have an obligation to break out of our self-made "bubbles" of friends, neighbors, and Internet algorithms that confirm everything we believe? If so, how can we do it? If not, can we still be effective participants in our democracy?

22. How do you think the common good can best be restored?

BEYOND OUTRAGE

What Has Gone Wrong with Our Economy and Our Democracy, and How to Fix It

America's economy and democracy are working for the benefit of ever-fewer privileged and powerful people. But rather than just complain about it or give up on the system, we must join together and make it work for all of us. The first step is to see the big picture. *Beyond Outrage* connects the dots, showing why the increasing share of income and wealth going to the top has hobbled jobs and growth for everyone else, undermining our democracy; caused Americans to become increasingly cynical about public life; and turned many Americans against one another. He also explains why the proposals of the "regressive right" are dead wrong and provides a clear roadmap of what must be done instead. Here's a plan for action for everyone who cares about the future of America.

Economics

AFTERSHOCK

The Next Economy and America's Future

When the nation's economy foundered in 2008, blame was directed almost universally at Wall Street bankers. But Robert B. Reich, one of our most experienced and trusted voices on public policy, suggests another reason for the meltdown. Our real problem, he argues, lies in the increasing concentration of wealth in the hands of the richest Americans, while stagnant wages and rising costs have forced the middle class to go deep into debt. Reich's detailed account of where we are headed over the next decades—and how we can fix our economic system—is a practical, humane, and much-needed blueprint for restoring America's economy and rebuilding our society.

Economics

REASON
Why Liberals Will Win the Battle for America

For anyone who believes that "liberal" isn't a dirty word but rather a term of honor, this book will be as revitalizing as oxygen. For in the pages of *Reason*, a former secretary of labor and one of our most incisive public thinkers mounts a defense of classical liberalism that's also a guide for rolling back twenty years of radical conservative domination of our politics and political culture. To do so, Robert B. Reich shows how liberals can shift the focus of the values debate from behavior in the bedroom to malfeasance in the boardroom, remind Americans that real prosperity depends on fairness, and reclaim patriotism from those who equate it with preemptive war-making and the suppression of dissent. If a single book has the potential to restore our country's good name and common sense, it's this one.

Political Science

ALSO AVAILABLE

The Future of Success
Locked in the Cabinet
The Resurgent Liberal
Saving Capitalism
Supercapitalism
The Work of Nations

VINTAGE BOOKS
Available wherever books are sold.
www.vintagebooks.com